Sharing and Caring Hands

My Mondays With Mary Jo Copeland

NANCY JO SULLIVAN

Liguori/Triumph
LIGUORI, MISSOURI

Imprimi Potest:
Richard Thibodeau, C.Ss.R.
Provincial, Denver Province
The Redemptorists

Published by Liguori/Triumph
An imprint of Liguori Publications
Liguori, Missouri
www.liguori.org
www.catholicbooksonline.com

Library of Congress Cataloging-in-Publication Data

Sullivan, Nancy Jo, 1956–
    Sharing and caring hands : my Mondays with Mary Jo Copeland / Nancy Jo Sullivan.—1st ed.
       p.   cm.
    ISBN 0-7648-0982-2
    1. Sullivan, Nancy Jo, 1956– 2. Christian biography—United States.
I. Title.

BR1725.S85A3 2003
248.4—dc21   2002043459

Printed in the United States of America
07 06 05 04 03   5 4 3 2 1
First edition

*This book is dedicated to
Mary Jo Copeland
and to the precious poor
she serves.*

Contents

Acknowledgments

I wish to extend my gratitude to the following people: To Mary Jo Copeland: Thanks for inviting me into the classroom of Sharing and Caring Hands. The lessons I learned from you will linger for many years to come. Your friendship is one of the greatest gifts of my life.

To Dick Copeland: Your devotion to Mary Jo and her work has blessed me. Truly, you are her "Knight in Shining Armor."

To the poor of Sharing and Caring Hands: During my ten Mondays at Sharing and Caring Hands, you took the time to welcome me, a stranger in your midst. That meant a lot to me.

To John Cleary, my editor: Many thanks for letting "my voice" come through in this manuscript. Your ongoing support enabled me to write this story from my heart.

To the entire Liguori team: It was a privilege to write this book for your company. You did more than just publish a book, you gave the poor an opportunity to speak.

To Connie Pettersen: You stayed up late, three nights in a row, to type and proofread the manuscript. Three cheers for you and for North Woods Transcription.

To Sarah, my daughter: You are my angel. Thanks for being such a good spiritual director. I'm so lucky God gave you to me.

To my precious family: I love you.

A Word From
Mary Jo Copeland

I hope this book helps you find God in your daily life. It is not what we say to God; it is what He says to us in the everyday moments of our lives. If we look, we will find Him. If we listen, we will hear Him. God is always present in both joy and sorrow. He wants us to turn to Him in our suffering, in our brokenheartedness, and to be grateful to Him in our joy. Take time to pray.

You will find great power, peace, and strength in prayer. We are all called to be channels of His peace and instruments of His love to all we live with and those who we meet on our journey. Jesus' mother Mary taught us much in saying yes to being the Mother of God. We are all called to be servants. God came to serve, not to be served. Can we do less?

May the peace of God and His Blessed Mother be with you all the days of your life.

Author's Note

Some of the names in this book have been changed to protect the dignity of the poor. In addition, some of the people I've written about are composites of two or three personalities. Nonetheless, each word, phrase, description, and conversation reflect the truth, as I experienced it, during my ten Mondays at Sharing and Caring Hands.

—NANCY JO SULLIVAN

Introduction

One of my favorite scriptural tales is nestled in the second chapter of the Luke. The story is about a man who is looking for God. Luke tells the story this way:

> Now there was a man in Jerusalem whose name was Simeon; this man was righteous and devout, looking forward to the consolation of Israel, and the Holy Spirit rested on him. It had been revealed to him by the Holy Spirit that he would not see death before he had seen the Lord's Messiah. Guided by the Spirit, Simeon came into the temple; and when the parents brought in the child Jesus, to do for him what was customary under the law, Simeon took him in his arms and praised God, saying, "Master, now you are dismissing your servant in peace, according to your word; for my eyes have seen your salvation..." (Lk 2:25–30).

When I reflect on this story, I try to imagine Simeon waiting in the temple that day. I picture him an aged, bearded, wrinkled man, sitting cross-legged on the stone floors of the temple, searching for God, praying fervently that he might see the savior's face before his days on earth come to an end. I can almost see him squinting as Mary and Joseph passed by, his aging eyes framed with crow's-feet, his vision fading. Did he turn his ear to hear the soft coos of the newborn baby that Mary carried in her arms? Why was he drawn to this family that he didn't even know?

It's clear that something miraculous happened when Simeon took little Jesus into his arms. He saw Christ. He touched the promised Messiah. He felt the unspeakable joy of God's promised presence. God opened his heart.

In our world today, there are "modern Simeons," good, God-fearing people who show us where to find God in our lives, how to see, hear, and touch the savior of the world.

One of those people is Mary Jo Copeland, the founder of Sharing and Caring Hands, a Minneapolis-based ministry which serves the needs of thousands of homeless and hungry people.

Several months ago, Mary Jo Copeland called me, asking if I would write a book about the poor. I had often seen Mary Jo Copeland on television, in newspapers and magazines. An unofficial "saint" to many, Mary Jo had received national recognition for years of charitable service which mirrored the work of Mother Teresa. Though I knew much about Mary Jo, the only thing she knew about me was that I was a Christian writer.

She didn't know that I was searching for God. She didn't know that I was a mother of three, that every minute of my day was scheduled, that my life revolved around kids and work deadlines and cleaning the house. In the busyness of my life, I longed to find time for God but it seemed impossible. Though my relationship with God had once been the center of my life, the constant rush of every day left little time for prayer, reflection, and quiet time. Like two estranged friends, the Lord and I had lost touch with one another. Was God still thinking about me? Was he still with me? I wondered.

After agreeing to write the book, I decided to spend ten Mondays at Sharing and Caring Hands. It was my intention to write an inspirational book which might bring more visibility to Mary Jo's ministry. What happened during those ten Mondays brought unexpected transformation to me. While watching Mary Jo care for the lost and lonely outcasts of this world, I started to see, clearly, the spiritual poverty in my own heart.

Like the poor, I was impoverished, but in a much different way. I was in need of the unseen wealth that can only be found in the human heart; the pearls of inner peace, the jewels of spiritual contentment, the diamonds of unwavering trust and faith.

Each Monday, I watched in wonder as Mary Jo touched the faces of the poor, looking into their eyes and sharing non-judgmental words of comfort. I don't recall the exact moment, but at some point, I began feeling God's presence in a way I never had before. At Sharing and Caring Hands, I started seeing the face of Christ in the faces of people, ordinary people who happened to be poor. God was speaking, I could hear his voice, clearly, as Mary Jo went about her daily work, encouraging the "family" God had given her, the brokenhearted, the homeless, the abandoned. Throughout the experience, I knew something miraculous was happening. God was renewing my faith. He was showing me where to look for his presence. I could find him, not only at Sharing and Caring Hands, but also in my own home and family, in the ordinary places and everyday faces that defined my busy life. God was opening my heart.

This book is about searching for God. It's about finding his promised presence in the people we see each day. It's about recognizing true poverty and reclaiming hope and unearthing the priceless treasure of God's unchangeable love.

May this book inspire you as you persevere on your journey of faith. It is my hope that as you read these pages, that you, like Simeon, will find God in your own life.

BLESSINGS,
NANCY JO SULLIVAN

ONE

Where Did God Go?

"Ask, and it will be given you; search, and you will find; knock, and the door will be opened for you."

MATTHEW 7:7

The clock in the upstairs hallway chimed 3:00 A.M. Outside our home, the winter winds of Minnesota moaned and howled. With my husband and three children fast asleep, I tiptoed down the stairs. Drawing near to a large living room window, I opened the drapes and shivered in my bathrobe. Though it was March, the last month of winter, cold drafts still seeped through the sill.

I turned on a small lamp. Peering through the glass panes, I watched as thick snowflakes tumbled and twirled like falling feathers. Fixing my gaze on our front yard lamppost, a beacon of light veiled in blowing snow, I sighed. I, too, was whirling in a never-ending storm of daily commitments and responsibilities. The demands of raising kids, keeping a home and balancing a career had obscured the light of God's presence in my life. "I miss you, God," I said softly.

It wasn't that I was dissatisfied with my life. Actually, I

was pretty content. On the brink of my middle-aged years, I was an author and editor for a major publishing company. With a steady stream of writing assignments, I had the luxury of working out of my home. Our family wasn't rich, but we lived in a modest two-story home and drove a two-year-old minivan. We had enough money to take summer vacations and buy two medium pizzas every Friday night.

Married to my husband, Don, for almost twenty years, our three daughters were "nice kids." Rachael, my freckled-face sixth grader, played hockey and soccer; she always sported a perpetual grin. Christina, dark-eyed and smart, was busy with high school and friends and tennis matches. "And Sarah, sweet Sarah," I whispered as my thoughts turned to my oldest child.

Soon, I heard the sound of soft, slippered footsteps coming down the stairs. "M-Mom? W-why are y-you awake?" a small voice stuttered. There was Sarah, my Down's syndrome daughter, standing on the landing. She must have heard me go downstairs. Though Sarah had just turned seventeen, she still bore a childlike sweetness. Wearing yellow pajamas, her reddish hair was curled into two ponytails. Her twinkling eyes sparkled behind pink-framed glasses.

"I can't sleep," I told her.

Though Sarah was limited in almost every area, she smiled constantly. A special education student at the local high school, we were proud of her humble accomplishments. With the help of some incredible teachers, Sarah had learned basic reading skills and she could write an assortment of words and phrases. Over the years, she had learned to dance and sing and play baseball. She loved fairy tales and flowing dresses and CDs of The Backstreet Boys and The Dixie Chicks.

"I...I want to b-be an actress s-someday," she often said.

The wind rattled against the living room window. Drawing near to my side, Sarah laid her head on my shoulder. "M-Mom...what's w-wrong?" she asked. Despite my daughter's disability, she was intuitive and wise—very wise. Sometimes I wondered if she was an angel. Time and again, I had shared my deepest struggles with Sarah. I valued her pure perspectives and her simple insights. Most of all, I cherished her honesty.

"I'm too busy...I can't find God," I told my daughter.

She nodded, carefully pondering my problem like she was a seasoned counselor. "W-where did God g-go?" she asked.

Sarah's question lingered as I began reviewing the previous day. That morning, I had gotten up at 5:30 for my regular morning workout. By 8:00, I had already driven the kids to school, cleaned the kitchen, paid some bills, and vacuumed out the car. After spending the rest of the morning typing an article at my home computer, I threw in two loads of wash and folded three.

The afternoon wore on as I drafted a short story and revised a chapter, all the while taking phone calls from my publisher. Later, after picking up the kids at school, I made Hamburger Helper on the stove while my girls did their homework at the kitchen table.

"Mom, I have hockey practice at 5:30," Rachael announced as she munched on an apple.

Christina looked up from her algebra book. "Mom, can we go shopping after dinner? I need a dress for the dance," she said.

Sarah just smiled as she paged through a book about Cinderella. The phone rang.

"I have a meeting tonight; I won't be home for dinner," my husband told me.

As I quickly served dinner on paper plates, Sarah watched my every move. "M-Mom…s-slow down," she said.

When at last the day came to a close, I collapsed on the couch in our family room, falling asleep to the sound of the ten o'clock news.

"I'm not sure where God went," I told Sarah as the two of us watched the wind blow funnels of snow around the outdoor lamppost. In the unrelenting rush of my life, the light of God's presence seemed hidden, concealed in the never-ending routines of my day.

I thought about the books I'd read on time management. "Change your schedule….Find creative ways to achieve your goals….Re-prioritize your life…," the authors suggested. I longed to find more time to pray, to worship, or just sit quietly before God.

"What can I change?" I asked myself. The truth was, most of my daily schedule was nonnegotiable. At this point in my life, my family needed me and, for the most part, I didn't begrudge the time I was giving them. "Enjoy this time…someday the kids will be gone," I often told myself. Quitting my job wasn't the answer. We needed the income. Besides, I loved writing. How could I make more time for God? What could I eliminate? My morning workout? Housework? Fixing meals?

"When you were a baby, I had lots of time for God." I told Sarah. I began remembering the early months of her life. Born with a congenital heart defect, we checked Sarah into the hospital when she was just six months old. After a risky heart surgery, Sarah was confined to a sterilized crib in the intensive care unit. A few hours after her operation, the doctors told us: "It doesn't look good."

That night, while nurses adjusted her breathing tubes and doctors wrote on clipboards, Don and I held Sarah's tiny hands. "Where are you, God?" I cried out. Though I was a new mother, I had little joy. "This is too hard. This isn't the way life is supposed to be," I angrily told my creator. It felt like I had been banished to a desert of hopelessness and despair.

As the weeks passed, the doctors continued to treat Sarah's ongoing infections. Meanwhile, my husband and I took turns keeping a round-the-clock vigil around her hospital crib. I took the "day shift."

Each morning, while nurses bathed our baby, I would make my way to the hospital chapel. There, I'd spend at least an hour in prayer, asking God for hope and healing. In the afternoon, while Sarah underwent tests and treatments, I would read devotionals by Henri Nouwen, Billy Graham, and Mother Teresa. In the evening, just before Don arrived for his nightly watch over Sarah, I would pour through bible passages and write in my journal.

Gradually, in the middle of that spiritual wasteland, God's presence began to burn like the bush that sustained Moses on the barren mountain. In that time of crisis, my daily routine revolved around prayer and faith and fellowship with God. I was close to God and he was close to me.

Now, so many years later, there was no major crisis in my life. The early burdens of Sarah's disability had been transformed into blessings, and I was grateful. Still, I wondered if it was possible to feel the burning fire of God's presence, even in the normal, everyday business of life.

"Sarah, I need to find God again," I said.

The two of us listened to the whining wind. Sarah tenderly patted my back. "M-Mom," she said. "Maybe God w-will find y-you."

TWO

Mary Jo's Rose

"Your smile and an outstretched hand is the beginning of a miracle in the unspoken need of another's heart."

MARY JO COPELAND

A few days later, on a Sunday afternoon, I found myself editing a manuscript at my computer. The phone rang.

"This is Mary Jo Copeland," a pleasant voice greeted. I immediately recognized the name. In Minnesota, Mary Jo Copeland is a household word. Many locals call her "The Mother Teresa of Minneapolis."

The founder of Sharing and Caring Hands, an outreach ministry that serves over twenty thousand people each month, I had read about Mary Jo in *Reader's Digest*, *Good Housekeeping*, and *The New York Times*. I knew that she was sixty, the mother of twelve grown children, and that her charity functioned on a never-ending budget of donations. A few months earlier, I had seen Mary Jo on CNN. In a nationally televised speech, President Bush had acknowledged Mary Jo as his friend.

"So good to hear from you," I said.

"Nancy, I've read your work. Will you write a book about the poor?" she asked.

At first, I wasn't sure what she was asking. "What kind of book?" I replied. Mary Jo began sharing a potpourri of stories about the people she knew so well, the homeless, the abandoned, the outcasts of society. "The poor have much to teach the world," she said.

As I held the phone, I scanned the mounds of paperwork that cluttered my nearby desk. I had planned to spend three months writing a collection of short stories; now half-finished manuscripts were piled everywhere and a twelve-page contract was waiting to be signed.

"Mary Jo, I'd love to write your book but I think I'm too busy," I said.

Mary Jo persisted. "Come see me tomorrow. I'll meet you in the cafeteria. We'll talk then," she said as she began giving me directions to Sharing and Caring Hands.

Later that night, I helped Sarah into bed, pulling a warm quilt over her shoulders. While my daughter folded her hands to pray, I couldn't stop thinking about Mary Jo.

"Sarah," I said, "do you think I should write a book about the poor?" I began telling my daughter about Mary Jo. "She helps people that don't have a house, she feeds people who are hungry, she takes care of people who are sad," I explained.

"D-does s-she h-help people f-find God?" Sarah asked.

"She does," I said, marveling at Sarah's intuition. Turning off her light, I made my way down the stairs. While I made the kids' lunches in the kitchen, thoughts of Mary Jo were still with me.

I can't write her book...I have too much to do. I rationalized that I couldn't put my own writing projects on hold, that there would be time to write for Mary Jo when the kids

were older. "It won't work," I whispered as I spread peanut
butter on bread. "I'd have to spend time at Sharing and Caring Hands, probably several mornings," I told myself as I
cut carrot sticks.

No, I couldn't do it. There just wasn't enough time.

"Say yes," a quiet, inner voice suggested.

As I put Oreos into baggies, I told myself that God was
fair. Surely he understood how busy I was. "Someone else is
supposed to write this book," I said aloud. But deep inside,
I couldn't help but wonder if that someone was *me*. I started
bargaining with God. "If you want me to do this, I'll need a
sign," I prayed. Even as I offered the petition, I knew that
my prayer sounded more like a business deal with God, a
deal that I would accept on my terms, not his.

Soon memories from my childhood began to surface. I
was in the second grade; it was just a few weeks before Easter. While the sun streamed into our classroom, I sat in a
front-row desk, surrounded by Catholic classmates. Sister
Claire, our religion teacher, stood by her desk, carefully ar-
ranging fresh red roses around a purple candle.

Dressed in a long black habit, Sister Claire's face was
wrinkled with age, but her eyes were warm and bright. "God's
love is like a rose," she said as she lit a candle. She began
explaining the ancient story of the cross, telling us about
the sufferings of Christ and the glories of his resurrection.
"The beauty of God's love will always overshadow the thorns
of our lives," she told us.

The flame flickered. Skinny strands of smoke rose from
the candle. The fragrance of rose petals filled the room like
perfume. "Let's pray that God will plant his love in our
hearts," she said.

After that day in second grade, I could never look at a

rose without thinking that I had caught a small glimpse of God.

The childhood memory faded. As I put the kids' lunches in the fridge, I prayed: "I'll do this if you send me a rose."

Early the next morning, I drove twenty-five miles of freeway into the inner city of Minneapolis. "It's a rough part of town," I told myself as I steered my minivan into the parking lot of Sharing and Caring Hands, a three-complex ministry, which included a large main building, a transitional apartment shelter, and an old storefront that had been turned into a day-care and teen center.

Peering through the windshield, I saw a long line of people waiting outside the main building which housed the cafeteria and offices. "Meet me by the cafeteria door; you'll see people gathered there," Mary Jo had told me.

I locked the doors of my minivan. I wished my kids hadn't piled hockey sticks and tennis rackets and shopping bags in the back seat. Here, in the inner city, these everyday items represented a lifestyle of financial security and, at least, moderate wealth. On this morning, I didn't want to look suburban or middle class. I wanted to blend in. I was glad I wore a hooded sweatshirt and blue jeans.

With quick steps, I walked past the line of people. I noticed that most of them were unkempt, all of them carrying something—a backpack, a baby, a bible. I felt uneasy. These were people that most of society would shun: a woman with rotting teeth, a crying man with a shaking disease, a teenager in a trench coat that smelled like cigarettes.

They watched me. I tried not to make eye contact. It wasn't that I felt better than them. I had known hard times, but had been spared the pain of hunger and homelessness.

"Nancy, so glad you could come," a nicely-dressed

woman said as she greeted me at the door that opened up to a large eating area with long tables.

Immediately, I knew the woman was Mary Jo. I recognized her from the magazine pictures I had seen. Wearing a flowered skirt and neatly ironed blouse trimmed with a cross pin, Mary Jo's shoulder-length hair was adorned with a shiny barrette. She looked like a professionally dressed businessperson, all except for her white bobbysocks and Adidas tennis shoes.

"Follow me, honey," she said. Taking my hand, she guided me into a kitchen where a group of volunteers had gathered to cook and serve the morning meal. "Let's pray," she said.

The volunteers, kids in private school uniforms and their parents, began forming a hand-holding circle around Mary Jo and me. "Lord, give us a heart of love," Mary Jo prayed as she cast her eyes toward heaven. "Bless the poor we serve," she added.

Mary Jo led me into the cafeteria, now swelling with 250 people. "Nancy, let me introduce you to some special friends," she said as we walked to a long table where a group of shabbily dressed people ate hot blueberry pancakes and slices of melon.

"Corrine, did you get enough to eat? Tyron, are you feeling better today? Otis, how's the bus driving job?" Mary Jo asked as she made her way around the table, all the while sharing handshakes and hugs and pats on the back. Mary Jo seemed so familiar with the people; she knew their names, their stories, their secret hurts and pains. "This is my friend, Nancy. She's an author," Mary Jo announced as she waved her hand at me like she was introducing me for an Academy Award.

"That's real nice," said a man wearing a skull and crossbones T-shirt.

"You should be real proud of yourself," said a scraggly-haired woman with wire rim glasses. My face turned red. I didn't want to be the center of attention.

We passed another table where three husky-looking men drank coffee from Styrofoam cups; all of them wore sleeveless shirts and had snake tattoos on their arms.

"Hello, boys. I've got some good news for you: God loves you," Mary Jo told the men.

I wondered if Mary Jo ever felt frightened. "Do you ever have crime here?" I asked, as I followed her out of the cafeteria and down a long hallway.

"Hardly ever. The poor take good care of me," Mary Jo said, unlocking her office door with the turn of a key. On a wall behind her desk were framed pictures of her family and an assortment of community service awards. A crucifix hung on a wall by a sunlight window.

Mary Jo's cell phone rang. "These darn phones! They take me away from God's work," she told me as she reached into her shirt pocket and clicked on her phone. I sat down on a nearby chair and chuckled. Mary Jo's life was not much different than mine; her days were filled with nonstop tasks and unexpected interruptions.

"Hello, Congressman," she told the caller. I listened as she talked about plans to build an orphanage in a nearby suburb. While I scanned her family photos, a tall distinguished-looking man in his early 60s peeked in and waved at Mary Jo. He was wearing khakis and a starched white shirt. Mary Jo put her hand over the phone. "Dick, this is Nancy. She's gonna write a book about the poor," she whispered.

The man waved. "Hello, I'm Mary Jo's husband, vice president of the ministry," he said. While Mary Jo continued her phone conversation, Dick explained that he assisted Mary Jo with most of the administrative aspects of Sharing and Caring Hands. "I'm off to a meeting. My office is right down the hall," he said. "Let me know if you need anything."

Mary Jo clicked off her phone. She pulled up a chair, right beside me, handing me a cup of coffee. "Nancy, you're the one to write this book. Will you be a voice for the poor?" she asked.

As she spoke, I suddenly felt as if I had known Mary Jo all my life. Though we barely knew each other, I had a sense that there was meaning in our meeting, that God had brought us to this place, at this time, for a very special purpose.

"Nancy, do you remember that story in the Bible, the one about Mary and Elizabeth?" Mary Jo asked.

I began recounting aloud the familiar scriptural tale. "The Virgin Mary—she was the Mother of God, and Elizabeth... wasn't she the mother of John the Baptist?" I asked.

Mary Jo nodded as if she knew something that I didn't. "They were just two ordinary mothers; good friends who said yes to God," Mary Jo explained. I remembered the ancient words that were spoken by the Blessed Mother of God so many years earlier; words which affirmed her willingness to accept God's plan. *"Here am I, the servant of the Lord."*

Like the Mother of God, it was clear that Mary Jo had already said yes to God. Even in the short moments that I had spent with her, I could tell that sharing and sacrifice and caring were part of her everyday life. She radiated humility and holiness. God was present in everything she said and did.

But me, my gifts were so much different than hers. I wasn't in a position to care for the poor like she was. I had a house to clean and children to raise and a daily job. Mary Jo was at a different stage of life. "God wants to use your writing abilities," Mary Jo told me.

My glance turned toward the crucifix. "I'll have to spend several mornings here. Mondays are best for me," I told her.

There it was. I was committed. There was no need for a heavenly sign. I had been sent here for a reason. There was something I needed to learn from Mary Jo and from the poor she served. "Yes, I'll write the book," I heard myself say.

Mary Jo's face lit up. "The poor will lead you to God," Mary Jo said. I watched as she pulled a small book from a nearby shelf and tucked a small card inside. "Here," she said, hugging me. "A little gift."

"I'll see you next Monday," I said.

As I drove home, I got caught in standstill traffic on the freeway. Lifting the book from my pocket, the small card fell onto the front seat. Taking it into my hand, I smiled. On the top edge of the card was a passage that read: "May grace and peace be yours in abundance."

Beneath the verse was a picture of a rose.

THREE

Home Is Where the Heart Is

"For where your treasure is, there your heart will be also."

LUKE 12:34

I have to meet Mary Jo at 8:15. We're leaving in five minutes," I called out from the kitchen as I put bagels in the toaster. The clock above the stove read 7:05. Don had just left for work. After a quick morning jog, I had somehow managed to squeeze in a shower and blow-dry my hair. Now dressed for the day in a purple wind suit, I helped Sarah zip up her coat and slip on her winter boots.

Christina and Rachael were getting ready upstairs; I could hear the sound of water running and toothbrushes tapping against the bathroom sink. "This house is a mess," I told Sarah as I handed her a bagel on a napkin. The night before, our family had made popcorn and watched old Shirley Temple movies. Now our kitchen counter was crowded with pans and bowls and opened cans of soda.

"Has anyone seen my car keys?" I hollered as I made my way to the family room where pillows and sleeping bags and kernels of popcorn still covered the carpet. Sarah followed me.

"This is no way to live," I muttered.

I was irritated. My house was a disaster. With all of us so busy, it would stay that way all day. "M-M-Mom, you need a m-maid," Sarah suggested as I discovered my keys on the mantle above the fireplace, right next to a row of family pictures that needed to be dusted.

I thought of a wealthy friend who had a housekeeper. "Now that would be the ultimate luxury; someone to clean my house," I said as I grabbed my jacket from the entryway closet. While Christina and Rachael raced down the stairs, scooping up their backpacks and boots from the closet, I handed them bagels to eat on the run.

Sarah reached for my purse; it was sitting on a nearby desk. "S-sorry, Mom," she said after she accidentally knocked a plaque off the wall and sent it tumbling to the floor.

I rolled my eyes. Sarah glanced downward and began slowly stuttering the words that were written on the plaque: "H-home is where the h-heart is," she said softly.

"Let's go," I said, an edginess in my voice. I gripped Sarah's hand as the four of us rushed off. We left the wall decoration lying on the floor.

About an hour later, I walked into the cafeteria of Sharing and Caring Hands. Crowds of street people were waiting to eat breakfast; they were talking to each other, their voices sounding like the background din of a lively reception. Weaving my way through the gathering, I saw Mary Jo standing in front of the large crowd. She was wearing a denim jumper and her tennis shoes squeaked when she walked.

"Be quiet...be still. Behave or be gone!" Mary Jo shouted to the crowd, a hint of firmness in her voice. A reverent hush fell over the cafeteria. I stopped in my tracks. "It's time for prayer. Prayer is the most important thing you will do today," Mary Jo said.

I looked around at the people who hemmed me in. On one side of me, a muscular man in a black T-shirt tenderly hoisted a toddler onto his massive shoulders. "Listen, son, Mary Jo's gonna talk about Jesus," he told the child.

To my left, a young teenage couple, a skinny girl in a midriff top and a gangly-looking boy with purple hair hugged each other and bowed their heads. In front of me, a woman in a black bowling jacket raised her hands. I could smell alcohol and cigarettes and Ivory soap, all at the same time.

"God loved us into life today and he promised he would be with us always," Mary Jo told the people.

I felt like I was in church. Mary Jo's mealtime prayer had the feel of a good sermon, a spiritual pep talk, a motivational speech designed to transform lives. "God loves you. He died on the cross for you," she said as she walked through the crowd, touching faces, gripping hands, and stroking hair. The poor listened to her every word; an endless sea of eyes meeting hers.

Mary Jo was a skilled preacher and Sharing and Caring Hands was her pulpit. With every spoken word, she was giving away a treasure-trove of hope. This was a welcoming place; Mary Jo made everyone feel as if they were in her living room. "The streets are hard, but you are never alone. Be at peace. God is with you and I am with you," Mary Jo said.

After the prayer, Mary Jo made her way to my side. "Nancy, I knew you would come. Let's go on a tour," she suggested. I followed her through the cafeteria doors and down a wide stairway. "Most of the people that come to

Sharing and Caring Hands are homeless," she said as we came to the bottom of the stairs. There I saw a private, enclosed area lined with ceramic tiled showers and sinks.

"A shower is one of the greatest gifts we can give to the poor. It's a small thing, but it can restore dignity to a broken person," Mary Jo said.

While she showed me shelves brimming with shampoo and shaving cream and Ivory soap, I thought of my upstairs bathroom. In my mind's eye I saw my kid's toothbrushes hanging on the wall. I imagined the towels and the washcloths that were neatly stacked in our linen closet. I could almost hear the sound of water running from our sink. "Bathrooms are luxuries," I thought to myself.

Most of the homeless don't have insurance; they can't afford to see a doctor," Mary Jo said as she led me down another hallway where county nurses and volunteer dentists were seeing patients in clean, sterilized rooms.

As Mary Jo unlocked a nearby door to a stocked food shelf, a man walked towards us, his face looked red and chapped from the cold winter winds. He was wearing only a thin, plaid shirt that was missing two buttons and he was limping.

"Mary Jo, I be needin' a warm jacket…it's cold out there," he said as he sniffed loudly. Mary Jo hugged him. "I'll help you," she said as she took his hand and showed him an adjacent room where tables were piled with donated clothing.

"What size do you wear, honey?" Mary Jo asked as she rummaged through the clothes, finally pulling out a used jacket with a fur-lined hood.

"Large or medium; it don't matter," the man replied.

Mary Jo helped him put on the coat. "God loves you.

Someday you will see him face to face," she said as she brushed his left cheek.

The man looked down as if he were embarrassed. "Thanks," he said. As he limped to a table filled with boxes of food, I saw him wipe away a tear.

"The homeless don't have kitchens or closets. To a needy person, a coat or a box of corn flakes is a priceless treasure," Mary Jo explained.

I thought about my house. That morning, I had left my home feeling irritated that there wasn't enough time to clean up the clutter. Now, as I watched a pregnant woman dig through a mound of used baby clothes, the only thing I felt was gratitude. I had a stove and refrigerator filled with food. I had an entryway closet full of winter jackets. I had heat and carpeting, running water and pretty drapes that hung on my windows.

"Mary Jo, I love my house; it's such a big part of me. I can't imagine not having a home," I told her.

Mary Jo began sharing a passage from Scripture; one that she had committed to memory. "Foxes have holes, and birds of the air have nests; but the Son of Man has nowhere to lay his head" (Luke 9:58), she said softly.

Though I had heard the passage many times before, I was hearing and understanding the words in a whole new way. "Jesus was homeless," I whispered. It was an amazing realization. God, the wondrous creator of all things, had no permanent address on earth.

My tour continued as I followed Mary Jo up the stairs and out the main doors of the cafeteria. We shivered in the winter winds as we ran across the snow-covered street to "Mary's Place," a transitional housing complex that had been named in honor of the Virgin Mary.

After a desk clerk buzzed us into a large and immaculate lobby area, Mary Jo began greeting tenants as they passed by; a young mother pushing a stroller, a little girl in a wheelchair, a teenage boy wearing an orange bandanna. I was beginning to realize that Mary Jo's passion for the poor was irrepressible. She wanted to stop and talk to *everyone*.

While Mary Jo took a child into her arms, I began reading a list of rules that were posted on the lobby walls:

> No alcohol or drug use
> All residents must be in their rooms at 9:00 P.M.
> Room checks occur each day between
>   10:00 A.M.–12:00 P.M.
> No theft or borrowing of property not given to you
>   will be tolerated

Beneath the rules was a large italicized note: *You are expected to work on finding housing in a diligent and aggressive manner. Finding a place to live is your number one priority.*

My glance turned towards a woman who was sitting on a bench; the left side of her face was bruised. "Mary Jo, what brought these people here?" I asked as we passed a glass-enclosed laundry room with several washersand dryers and soda machines.

"Bad relationships, bad addictions, bad credit, bad choices…," Mary Jo replied.

While we took an elevator to the second floor, she told me that Mary's Place provided a safe, clean location for people in need to refresh their souls. "God is good. He wants to bring wholeness to our lives. He loves everyone, regardless of their past," Mary Jo said as the elevator door opened.

Soon we came to an apartment where the door was partially opened. "Can we come in for just a minute?" Mary Jo asked as a young Native American woman and her two small daughters greeted us with warm smiles.

"Mary Jo! Mary Jo!" the children shouted as they jumped up and down with glee. I assumed the family was just moving in; there were three cardboard boxes on the living room floor, all of them filled with humble belongings: family photos, a few pieces of clothing, and some toys.

Mary Jo knelt down and began helping the youngest of the children place a framed family picture on a table. I looked around. The living room was furnished with clean couches and chairs. The kitchen looked fully stocked with pots and pans and appliances. Glancing down the hall, I saw two bedrooms with bunk beds dressed in crisp white linens.

"This is our old house," the little girl told Mary Jo as she pointed to the family photograph. I drew near and took at peek at the photo. I saw what looked to be a smiling mother and father sitting on a couch, hugging their children. Behind the couch, pictures of the kids hung on the wall and a warm fire crackled in the fireplace. I wondered what had happened to this family. Where was the father? Had he left them? How had they lost their home? For just a moment, I allowed myself to imagine myself in this woman's place. How frightened she must be.

"Let's ask Jesus to help you find another home," Mary Jo told the child. As Mary Jo linked hands with the homeless family, I felt uncomfortable. I didn't know the secret hurts of this family. Would they take offense if I joined in their private circle of prayer? My hesitations quickly disappeared as the mother extended her hand to me.

"Our Father, who art in heaven, hallowed be thy name," Mary Jo began.

"Thy kingdom come, thy will be done, on earth as it is in heaven," I prayed fervently. This family, like all families, deserved the comfort and security of a permanent home.

"Give us this day, our daily bread, and forgive us our trespasses as we forgive those who trespass against us," the mother said, her voice trembling. I watched as her two daughters reached up to dab away their mother's tears.

"And lead us not into temptation, but deliver us from evil, for thine is the kingdom, the power, and the glory," Mary Jo said. She squeezed the mother's hand tightly.

For the rest of the morning, I sat with Mary Jo in the lobby of the apartment complex. I watched and listened as she interviewed an endless stream of families who needed shelter from abuse, addiction, and eviction. No matter what the circumstances, Mary Jo offered each family dignity. She touched their faces, their hands.She looked into their eyes. Sometimes she cried with them. "God makes his home in your heart," she told each one.

When morning was over, Mary Jo walked me to my car.

"Mary Jo, you have found God in the hearts of the homeless," I said. I almost envied her closeness to God. She was doing God's work, every minute, every hour of the day. "I'm not able to do what you do," I told her.

Mary Jo helped me open my car door. "Nancy, you're not called to do what I do," she said. She turned and scurried back to the apartment building, the cold wind flecked with snow. "Go home, Nancy. Look for God there!" she shouted.

Later that day, the kids and I began our regular afternoon routine of picking up the house. While Sarah cranked up her favorite songs on her CD player, Christina and Rachael cleaned up the family room.

"Mom, you don't need a maid," Christina said as she rolled up sleeping bags.

"You have us," Rachael added as she dusted the family photos above the fireplace.

I chuckled as Sarah and I began to re-hang the wall plaque in the hallway. As the two of us stood back to assess if it was straight, Mary Jo's words echoed in my mind: "Go home…look for God there."

I turned and glanced at the rooms that surrounded me, the kitchen, the living room, the stairway, the bathrooms, the family room. I thought about Mary Jo. Sharing and Caring hands was a sacred refuge where each day people found food and shelter and spiritual refreshment. It was a holy place—her "church."

My home is my church. Whether cluttered or clean, it too was a refuge; a place where my soul and the souls of my family were constantly being renewed. Even though my home didn't have stained-glass windows or baptismal fonts or wooden benches, it had pretty curtains and comfy couches where I could cuddle up with the kids and listen to the happy music that often played from Sarah's radio.

My home had closets brimming with warm garments and water that flowed from kitchen sinks, and bathroom showers and a washing machine that still worked—even after a decade of constant use.

It had holy places where daily bread was often passed and shared; morning bagels eaten in the entryway, popcorn munched in the family room, speedily cooked dinners served at the kitchen table. These simple gifts sanctified our lives and brought dignity to our days. I could no longer overlook the wonders of these everyday gifts. Even in the business of my life, I could learn to offer praise—daily praise for these precious provisions.

"God, you are here in my house. Help me to recognize and appreciate your presence in the simplest things…help me to teach my children to do the same," I silently prayed.

"M-Mom, it's straight. L-let's read it," Sarah said as she began gently guiding her hand over the wall plaque. At first, I stood in silence, staring at the plaque and quietly reflecting on the unforgettable lessons I had learned that morning at Sharing and Caring Hands.

"God lives in our home," I told Sarah. She nodded as if I was sharing old news. Our voices blended as we slowly and carefully mouthed the words that were written on the plaque, words that now sounded like a heaven-sent message:

"H-home is w-here the h-heart is."

FOUR

Saints in Training

"It's not time that makes a saint, it's the will."
MARY JO COPELAND

I t was sunny that first Monday in April. Outside, patches of grass were now beginning to replace the snowy land-scape that had covered our neighborhood for almost six months. As I drove the kids to school, I could feel the first rays of Spring warm my face through the windshield.

With the girls not quite awake, the car was quiet. I drove down the interstate and felt my thoughts drifting. Now that I was in my mid-forties, I was beginning to realize how swiftly the years were passing. *The kids are growing up. There's still so much I want to do with my life.*

Soon my children began chattering, breaking into my thoughts.

"Mom, I need new soccer shoes," Rachael called out from the backseat. "Mom, I have driver's training after school. Can you pick me up a little later?" Christina added.

While I grabbed my sunglasses from the dashboard, Sa-rah dug into her backpack and pulled out a field trip form. "M-Mom, you h-have to s-sign this. I need $8.00 for the Science Museum," she said.

I drove onward, trying to steer the car and read Sarah's form at the same time. The kids kept sharing thoughts and making requests and asking questions.

"Mom, Mom, Mom. Do you kids realize how many times a day you use that word?" I asked.

Didn't they know I had a name before I became a mother? Didn't they understand that I was more than a "mom"; that I was a person, a creative person with hopes and dreams for the future?

Sometimes raising my kids seemed like a repetitive regime of mundane tasks and never-ending demands. Most of my daily hours were spent in the car, the kitchen, or at the computer.

My world is so small!

I wanted to tell my kids that I often envisioned myself owning a secluded cabin where I could write a best-selling novel without any interruptions. I wanted to let them know that I was planning on running a marathon before I got too old; that I often dreamed about traveling to Ireland; and that sometimes I secretly wondered what I would look like as a blonde.

Sarah waved her hands in dismay. "But Mom, you're a m-mother…and that's a g-good th-thing," she said emphatically.

I looked in the rearview mirror. Christina and Rachael were trying to hold back their giggles.

After dropping the kids off, I arrived at the cafeteria of Sharing and Caring Hands just as the morning meal was being cleared and the volunteers were wiping down the tables. Though breakfast was over, many of the poor still lingered in the cafeteria, some of them now beginning to form an orderly line along one of the walls. Mary Jo stood at the front of the line surrounded by a few volunteers who held clipboards and small pads of paper. Holding a bucket brimming with handmade rosaries, Mary Jo motioned me near. She placed the bucket into my hands.

"Nancy, each morning I talk with the people. If I can, I help them; I know what it's like to be hopeless," she said.

Even though the line was growing longer, Mary Jo gently pulled me aside. "Let me tell you about my past," she said. Mary Jo began remembering her childhood years, painful years filled with neglect and abuse. "My mother often left me alone. I was always dirty. I had no friends. I often felt afraid," she said.

Mary Jo revealed that as a little girl, she spent many hours praying alone in her neighborhood church. "I dreamed of being a saint," she began. I told God that if I couldn't be a saint, I would be a nun. Instead, I married Dick and we had twelve children," she said.

Mary Jo and I doubled over with laughter, our chortles ripping through the crowded cafeteria like music that was turned up too loud.

"Mothers and saints…aren't they the same thing?" I asked with a chuckle.

"They are," Mary Jo replied. Still giggling, she turned to take her place at the front of the line.

"What do I do with these?" I shouted as I held up the bucket of rosaries.

"Give 'em away," she said.

I held my head high. I had a job to do. Taking my place at a nearby table, I began passing out the colorful rosaries made from twine and plastic beads.

From where I sat, I could hear Mary Jo answer nonstop questions and relentless requests for food, shoes, bus vouchers, dental care, diapers, and temporary shelter.

"Mary Jo, my shoes are worn out…Mary Jo, I'm behind in my rent…Mary Jo, my baby is sick…," came the countless pleas. With each story, Mary Jo nodded her head as if she understood. She offered motherly comfort and concrete solutions. Sometimes she motioned for volunteers to give away shoes or write out checks for the poor. Every financial gift was carefully recorded on paper by trained volunteers.

I watched as a teenage girl approached Mary Jo with a broad grin. Her dark hair was pulled back into a long braid, her face trimmed with glitter. She looked to be about six months pregnant. Wearing a white maternity top, the teenage mother-to-be had a simple request.

"Mary Jo, would you bless my baby?" she asked.

With gentle reverence, Mary Jo placed her hand on the young girl's rounded tummy. I watched as the two women, one young, one older, closed their eyes and prayed quietly, their foreheads touching.

Biblical images began surfacing in my mind's eye. I couldn't help but remember Luke's tender account of another teenage mother who received a similar blessing. I recalled how Mary, young and pregnant with the Son of God, traveled to see her older cousin Elizabeth. I could almost picture Elizabeth's greeting to Mary: "Blessed are you among women, and blessed is the fruit of your womb." I sensed that I was watching a re-enactment of the ancient biblical tale.

Next in line was a slender man who wore an outdated jacket with holes in the sleeves. He kept looking at the floor as he drew near to Mary Jo.

"Can I make a long-distance phone call?" the man asked; his voice choked with emotion.

"What's wrong, honey?" Mary Jo asked. She tenderly patted his cheek.

"My mom's in the hospital…Rochester…Mayo Clinic…," he said.

Mary Jo motioned for a volunteer. "Show this man the phone. Give him a bus ticket to the Mayo Clinic and a little extra money," she said.

As the volunteer led the downcast man to a private office area, Mary Jo called out: "And throw in a picture of Jesus, too!"

Mary Jo…Mary Jo…Mary Jo…. It seemed like every few seconds someone was calling out her name. *She's a mother to too many.* I thought about how many times a day my children used the word "mother." *How does Mary Jo keep on doing this, day after day?*

"Let's pray," Mary Jo shouted when the pleas for help became overwhelming. Though she sounded like a drill sergeant commanding a large troop, the entire line of people bowed their heads. As Mary Jo led them in the Lord's Prayer, no one seemed to mind taking time to implore the help of God.

After the prayer, a handsome man in his mid-twenties, a nicely dressed guy wearing a Tommy Hilfiger jacket, stepped to the front of the line. He was chewing on a toothpick; his head tilted to the side like a famous movie star.

"Mary Jo, I need some new tennis shoes," he said, his request sounding more like a demand. Mary Jo looked him up and down like he was part of a police lineup. She stared at his leather boots.

"God gave you an able body. Go and get a job. You can earn those tennis shoes," she told him in a stern maternal tone. He walked away like a scolded child.

"Mary Jo," I asked as she moved past my table on her way to the next needy person. "How do you know when to say no?"

She smiled. "I'm a mother. I can read people's hearts," she said. While Mary Jo continued working the line, I was amazed as I watched her carefully discern who needed help and who didn't. "McDonalds down the street is hiring; you'll make $6.00 an hour," I often heard her say.

Soon a little boy drew near my table. As I helped him put a rosary around his neck, I found myself wondering about the years Mary Jo had spent mothering twelve children. Surely in raising so many kids, Mary Jo had mastered the art of tending to the endless needs of the people she now served.

Maybe motherhood is a training ground for saints.

The little boy tugged at my arm, prying me away from my thoughts. "Who is this?" he asked, as he pointed to the plastic cross that trimmed his rosary. His eyes were chocolate brown, full of endearing curiosity. I looked closely at the cross. There, molded into the plastic was a tiny etching of Christ, nails in his hands and feet.

"That's Jesus," I told the boy.

The child brushed his small hands over the cross. "Jesus...I know him!" the boy cried out.

"You do? How do you know him?" I replied.

The brown-eyed boy hopped on top of a chair so that he could stand above me like he was on a stage.

"Mary Jo told me about Jesus. He died on a cross...but we shouldn't be sad," the child said. He could barely catch his breath; he was so excited to share everything that Mary Jo had told him. Now most of the people in line were watching him. "Jesus…he rose from the dead…and we should be happy!" the boy shouted.

The little boy, wearing the rosary, was waving his hands in the air, mimicking the glorious resurrection of Christ.

Mary Jo drew near and hugged and kissed the child like he was her own son. With the tenderness of a mother, she took his face in her hands and said, "When you get to heaven, Jesus will say, 'I know you, too,'" she said.

The morning hours passed as Mary Jo continued to work her way through the line. When noontime came, Mary Jo rushed to my side. "It's time to pray over the lunchtime meal," she said.

I handed her the bucket of rosaries. "Thanks for letting me pass these out. I've got to run too; Sarah has a doctor's appointment," I told her.

Mary Jo's life was like mine. Each minute of her life was slotted into a swiftly moving schedule. While Mary Jo walked me to the exit, I wondered if she ever grew tired of being a mother to so many. She was retirement age. Did she ever think about moving into a maintenance-free town house, playing golf by the ocean, or traveling to a foreign country?

"Mary Jo, do you ever dream of doing something else?" I asked.

"There's nothing else I'd rather be doing. Each day, when I care for the poor, I'm meeting Jesus," she said as she hugged me good-bye. "Nancy," she added, "God is present in the mundane."

Later that evening, I sat on the sidelines of a soccer field waiting for Rachael to finish practice. While my husband played tennis with Christina on a nearby court, Sarah sat by my side.

"M-Mom...how d-did it go with M-Mary Jo?" she asked. She wanted to hear all about it.

"Sarah, Mary Jo let me pass out rosaries. I brought you one," I said. Reaching into my purse, I pulled out a yellow rosary and handed it to her.

"Oh-hh...it's b-beautiful," she said. I watched as she ran her hands over the beads like she had just received a price-less jewel. "That's Jesus. You know him," I said as I pointed to the plastic cross that trimmed the holy strand. Sarah smiled.

I thought back to my morning. Mary Jo had shown me that motherhood was a greater calling than owning a cabin or writing a novel or running a marathon. Even though these dreams were worth pursuing—and in time I would pursue them all—they were temporal dreams. Motherhood, on the other hand, was preparing me for heaven.

The daily tasks of driving my kids to school, buying them soccer shoes and writing out checks for field trips had eter-nal significance. In caring for my daughters, even in simple ways, I was learning patience and compassion. Like Mary Jo, I was living out a vocation of love. Each day, I was meet-ing Jesus in my kids and he was meeting me.

I am blessed among women.

Just then, Rachael and Christina ran towards me, one carrying a soccer ball, the other toting a tennis racket. "Mom, let's go out for ice cream," Christina begged, her long hair pulled back into a ponytail.

"Mom, can we? Please...please?" Rachael added as she tossed her soccer ball into the air.

Sarah began mimicking the words I had spoken that morning: "M-Mom, Mom, M-Mom...i-is that the only w-word you k-know?" she said, her tone both smug and sweet.

I dug into my purse and retrieved a "two for one" coupon for Dairy Queen. Teasing the girls, I began waving the coupon high above my head.

I looked at my girls' faces. They were laughing, jumping like fish to snatch the coupon out of my hand. In that mundane moment of motherhood, one of so many, I felt God smiling on us.

Here on this soccer field, he was training me for eternity. Though my world was small, and my schedule busy, Mary Jo had helped me to discover a great spiritual truth.

God is present in monotony.

I vowed that I would look for God each day, in mundane places like my kitchen, my van, even my home computer.

"Sarah," I said as I tucked the coupon in her hands. "I'm a mother. I will always be a mother...and that's a good thing."

For God So Loved...

"I want to bring prayer to the country before I go home to God...where there is prayer, there is hope."

MARY JO COPELAND

I tucked Sarah into bed that Sunday evening, her bedside light shining dimly. Christina and Rachael lounged nearby on the carpet; their outstretched legs and arms surrounded by Sarah's stuffed animals. While my husband watched a hockey game downstairs in the family room, the girls and I shared "small talk," chattering about the upcoming week.

"Tomorrow morning," I said, "I have to get up at 3:30. I'm going to meet Mary Jo for prayer."

Christina gasped. "3:30 A.M.?" she asked, her dark eyes widening.

"For prayer?" Rachael bellowed.

I began telling them what little I knew about Mary Jo's daily prayer routine. "She prays at her church; two hours every morning. I want to write about it," I said.

Sarah pointed to an extra bed. "M-mom, sleep h-here tonight. M-my clock w-will w-wake you," she said. She

35

waved her hand at an elephant-shaped clock that was ticking on her dresser.

I set the alarm. The girls kept teasing me. "You'll be holy when you come home," they said laughing. They joked about a scene from the classic movie *The Ten Commandments*—the famous scene where Moses journeys to the top of Mount Sinai to meet God.

"You'll find God at Mary Jo's church; your face will glow," Christina said.

"You'll be like Moses...you'll see a burning bush...your hair will turn white," Rachael added, waving her hands to imitate a wild flame.

I rolled my eyes as Christina and Rachael rushed off to their rooms to do homework. I could hear them laughing all the way down the hallway.

"M-Mom, they b-bug m-me, too," Sarah said with a giggle.

I made the Sign of the Cross on my daughter's forehead. I recalled a night when Sarah was about nine. I was sitting at her bedside, tucking her in, our usual nighttime routine. At that time, her speech skills were beginning to improve and I decided it was time to teach her a simple prayer, one about God and guardian angels.

I recited each line slowly enough that young Sarah could follow along.

"It's...it's...t-too h-hard for m-me," my nine-year-old daughter admitted. She sighed in dismay. Stroking her hair, I saw her brow wrinkle with frustration.

"Sarah, what do you want to tell God?" I asked.

Sarah closed her eyes tightly as if formulating her thoughts. After a few moments of silence, she muttered the words: "Dear God...I...I...love m-my mom."

Throughout the years, Sarah had offered the same "mom-prayer" each night before she fell asleep. It was a simple, unpretentious prayer that always made me feel special.

"I am loved," I had told myself each time I heard my handicapped child pray. Now that she was almost eighteen, I listened, once again, to her precious petition.

"Sarah, I think you are an angel," I said as I kissed her goodnight. She laughed and closed her eyes. I crawled into the extra bed and fell asleep.

The next morning, at 3:29 A.M., I awoke to the staticky roar of Sarah's elephant alarm.

While my family slept, I got dressed and slipped down the stairs and out the front door. As I drove to Mary Jo's church, a journey of thirty-five minutes from my home, a gentle rain fell on my windshield. There wasn't anyone on the road and I could hardly keep my eyes open.

Mary Jo prays at this hour, every morning—how does she do it?

Even as I asked the question, I felt guilty. I knew that a regular "prayer time" was important. Though I often uttered "on the run" prayers while doing the wash or writing at my computer, my daily schedule was packed. Finding a block of uninterrupted time to pray each day seemed impossible.

My thoughts drifted back to the first months of Sarah's life. I remembered the many hours I spent by her hospital crib-side, keeping a constant, prayerful vigil. Though I was overwhelmed with doubt and despair, her hospital room was often quiet and still. Back then I spent lots of time looking at a crucifix that hung above her sterilized metal crib. In that time of uncertainty, there was nothing to do but "receive" the comforting presence of God.

"That was then," I said, as I pulled into the parking lot of Mary Jo's church. Waiting for me in the church entryway were Mary Jo and her husband Dick. Even though it was dark and rainy, a light above the main doors lit their silhouettes.

"I'm glad you didn't get lost," Mary Jo said, her rain-drenched hair clipped with bobby pins. Dick opened the church doors with a key that the pastor had given them. "I'll be your tour guide this morning," he joked.

Though Dick was often in Mary Jo's shadow, the man who ran the bureaucratic aspects of the ministry, his devotion to Mary Jo was obvious. On many occasions, I had seen him helping Mary Jo at Sharing and Caring Hands. He often met with the poor in his office, counseling them and providing them with support. Sometimes he even helped Mary Jo wash feet.

"Dick prays with me every morning," Mary Jo said as we entered the dimly lit church.

I followed Mary Jo and Dick to a small alcove in the back; it was lined with brick walls and votive candles that burned in tall blue glasses.

"Mary Jo begins each morning here," Dick explained as his wife began lighting candles. He went on to explain that each candle represented a specific prayer request. "Sometimes she lights a candle for the poor and asks God to end their suffering," Dick said. "Other times she lights candles for loved ones: her children, her friends, even those strangers she has promised to pray for," Dick added.

Mary Jo overheard our whispers, several candles now burning before her. "Today, I'm praying that all the souls in the world will find God," she said softly, her face aglow from the small flames.

Dick and I looked on as the candles flickered, their brightness reflecting like stars on the brick wall.

"What about you, Mary Jo? Do you ever light a candle for yourself?" I asked. In the last few weeks, I had seen her pour out more love on the poor than seemed humanly possible. Even though her energy seemed to come straight from heaven, and I had heard many people call her a saint, deep down I knew she was as human as I was.

"Everyday I ask that God will make me a vessel of his love," Mary Jo said, as she knelt down on a padded kneeler. Folding her hands, she bowed her head in quiet prayer. Dick took a place in the back row pew. The rain fell softly on the roof of the church.

I sat on a nearby chair. I tried to embrace the holiness of that moment, but my thoughts began to wander. I thought about all the things that I needed to do that day. Would I have time later in the day to finish a manuscript? Was there hamburger in the fridge for dinner? Would I be able to squeeze in a haircut? What time was Sarah's school conference? Did the kids need a ride anywhere?

I looked towards Mary Jo, her candlelit silhouette looking like a beautiful still-life painting. In just a few hours, she would be working at Sharing and Caring Hands. People would be waiting for her there, all of them lined up with desperate needs. Like me, her day would soon be filled with chatter and movement and ringing phones. Yet here, while the rest of the world slept, she was kneeling in silence. Here in the stillness, something sacred was happening. I could feel it. God's presence—his divine love—was here, hovering.

Just receive, an inner voice whispered. I fixed my gaze on the burning candles. I could hear the patter of rain on the roof. I closed my eyes. My preoccupation with the day ahead began to fade. In that moment, nobody needed anything from me. I had God's undivided attention and he had mine. God was pouring out his love to me, like the rain shower that fell outside the church. The only thing I needed to do was receive it.

Several minutes passed. While I continued to relish the sacred silence, Mary Jo made the Sign of the Cross and quietly slipped away to another open area in the back of the church.

"Let's follow her," Dick whispered as he led me to another alcove. There two tall candles in brass holders burned like torches. In the light of those candles, Mary Jo knelt before a life-size crucifix that hung on the brick wall. "Every morning, Mary Jo prays before the cross," Dick said.

I didn't want to intrude on Mary Jo's space, but I was starting to believe that she knew a lot more about prayer than I did. I wanted to learn from her.

"Would she mind if I joined her?" I asked Dick.

"She would like that," he replied.

While Dick leaned against a wall, keeping his own prayer vigil, I drew near to the crucifix and knelt right next to Mary Jo.

"Nancy, look at the cross. You will see the suffering of the poor," Mary Jo said.

I gazed at the stone sculpture that was nailed to the cross. Looking at the chiseled lash marks on Christ's face, I began seeing the faces of the people I had met at Sharing and Caring Hands, hundreds of them; children, unwed mothers, hard-looking men, women trying to start new lives.

They are all suffering, just like Jesus. I fixed my gaze on the nails in Christ's hands. *Homelessness, abuse, addiction, these are all nails that wound the poor....* My glance turned to the crown of thorns. *Each day, the hearts of the poor are being pricked with the thorns of doubt and despair.*

The rain continued to fall, pounding on the church rafters like drumbeats. I kept looking at the cross. Soon a passage from Scripture surfaced, one that I had memorized years earlier: "For God so loved the world that he gave his only son..." (Jn 3:16).

I took a deep breath, as if I was inhaling holiness. *Mary Jo loves the poor...like Jesus.*

Dick drew near and handed his wife a rosary. "You left this by the votive candles," he told her, his large shadow casting an angelic-looking image on the candlelit wall.

Mary Jo squeezed his hand. "Thanks, Honey," she told him.

Rosary in hand, Mary Jo got up and made the Sign of the Cross. Then she began walking around the aisles of the church, her gait swift and sure. While quietly mouthing words of prayer, she turned corners around the pews, waving her arms like she was competing in a race. Dick and I watched from the back of the church. "When the doctor told Mary Jo that she needed to exercise, she started wearing tennis shoes to church," he said.

I chuckled. "She power-walks and prays?" I asked. Dick just laughed.

It occurred to me that even though Mary Jo was busy, she had found a creative way to spend regular time with God. By combining daily prayer with exercise, she was utilizing her time wisely. In giving God the first hours of her day, she was receiving both physical and spiritual benefits.

I thought about the hour I spent each morning working out. *I can do that, too.*

Mary Jo continued her vigorous prayer walk while Dick and I sat down and talked quietly.

"Do you pray as much as Mary Jo does?" I asked.

Dick took off his glasses and rubbed his eyes. I was surprised to find him fighting back tears. "I'm not as holy as Mary Jo. I only pray one simple prayer every day. I ask God that I can be with Mary Jo her whole life and that she would die in my arms. I would not want her to be alone," he said, sniffling.

I was at a loss for words. Dick's love for Mary Jo was a prayer in itself.

Later that morning when I arrived home, I made my way to a storage closet in the family room. Pulling a cardboard box from the top shelf, I found a wooden crucifix; an old wedding gift that I had never found the right place for. Blowing away puffs of dust, I hung the cross on a wall above my computer. *I'll take time to look at it each day.*

A few hours later, I picked up the kids from school. With Sarah sitting next to me in the front seat, Christina and Rachael joked from their seats in the rear of the van. "Look at Mom's face...she saw a burning bush at Mary Jo's church...her face is glowing," they teased.

"I did see fire," I told them. The kids listened intently as I explained all that I had learned about prayer. "Each day, Mary Jo lights candles for those she loves," I told them.

Sarah looked back at her sisters. "See, M-Mom did see...see fire," she snapped.

The afternoon hours wore on as I made dinner in the kitchen. While I opened a box of fish sticks, I made a commitment to combine my morning workout with prayer and quiet reflection. *I'll be a good steward of my time. I'll start tomorrow.*

At the close of the day, I found myself at Sarah's bedside, tucking her in as I had so many nights before. "Dear God...I...I...love my mom," Sarah prayed.

I closed my eyes. *All prayer is an expression of love.* Now I understood why Mary Jo prayed for two hours each morning. *Prayer is receiving God's love, seeing God's love, and sharing God's love with others.*

As I turned out Sarah's light, I could hear the elephant clock ticking. I closed my eyes. Though I spoke no words, I knew my heart was offering an eloquent prayer. "Dear God...I love Sarah."

SIX

A Reason to Rejoice

*"I'm like a loose cannon, if you want to know
the truth. When you have boundless love, it's
like a fire in the forest, like water in a river, it's
hard to stop."*

MARY JO COPELAND

The morning sunrise was colored with pink streams
of light. Sitting on our front porch, I tied my jog-
ging shoes and set my sports watch for one half-hour.
Reaching into the pocket of my sweatpants, I pulled out a
small bible. Though a week had passed since I had observed
Mary Jo at her church, her words of wisdom still lingered in
my memory: *"Take time for prayer each day…that's how you
will find God."*

Now on this Monday morning, I had gotten up a few
minutes earlier for my morning jog. I was excited to follow
Mary Jo's lead, combining exercise with prayer and reflection. I had decided that each morning, I would read one
brief passage from Scripture. *I'll think about the verse while I
jog.…*

I opened the Bible and began reading: "Rejoice in the
Lord always" (Phil 4:4).

Pondering the passage, I set out for my run. While my tennis shoes crunched over the gravel on the road, I reflected back on times in my life when I had "experienced true rejoicing." Happy images began surfacing in my memory; the day I was married, the morning Sarah recovered from a life-threatening surgery, the afternoon my first book arrived in the mail.

"Rejoice...always...," I whispered. I was skeptical. *Joy is for special occasions.*

I turned a corner, passing a clump of wild flowers. I smelled the subtle fragrance of roses as my swift footsteps surged forward. "My life is like this jog," I mused. Each day, I raced through a path of schedules and commitments. I kept a steady pace, preoccupied with ordinary things; mothering, writing, keeping house. My life was filled with goodness; still, I rarely took time to notice, to acknowledge, to "feel" the beauty of God's presence in my life.

I'm too busy to rejoice.

A few minutes later, I was rushing around the kitchen, fixing breakfast for the kids. While Sarah helped me put waffles in the toaster, Rachael and Christina sat at the kitchen table arguing.

"You wore my shirt last night. You didn't wash it," Christina snarled.

Rachael made a face at her sister and replied, "You wore my skirt last Tuesday. I found it crumpled underneath your bed."

The night before, Christina and Rachael had stayed up too late. I knew they were tired and edgy; both of them had bags under their eyes. I opened the fridge and took out a bottle of syrup. The arguing continued.

"That's it!" I called out. I pointed to the kitchen sink

where plates were piled. "Before you two eat wash the dishes," I stammered.

While Christina and Rachael began scrubbing pans, Sarah and I ate waffles at the table. Through thick-lensed glasses, Sarah studied the look of dismay on my face.

"M-Mom, are y-you h-happy today?" she asked.

I wasn't sure how to answer her question. My daily life was so ordinary; each minute was filled with routine tasks like fixing meals and diffusing arguments and driving the kids to school. "Look for God in the mundane," Mary Jo had told me. Was it really possible to "rejoice always," to feel the "joy of the Lord" in the unremarkable moments of life? I wondered.

Later that morning, when I arrived at Sharing and Caring Hands, I parked my minivan outside a large door marked "Donation Drop-off." I saw Mary Jo greeting well-to-do people as they dropped off boxes of used clothing and household goods. Drawing near, I noticed a middle-aged man stacking donations on a nearby shelf. His busy hair was gray and he wore a T-shirt logoed with a happy face.

"That's Larry," Mary Jo said. She went on to explain that Larry had once been a mailman in the suburbs. "When Larry retired, he decided to help me," Mary Jo said.

He waved at me, laughing like Santa Claus. "It's a great day," he said as he unloaded a box of donated soap.

Soon a well-groomed woman, about sixty years old, drove up to the donation dock. With her skin tanned from years in the sun, the woman carried a box of clothing and dropped it front of Mary Jo. "I've been making donations for ten years and no one has ever acknowledged me!" the woman said as she angrily stomped her foot. She looked and sounded like a small child having a temper tantrum.

Mary Jo turned to Larry and whispered, "Quick, go upstairs: there's some flowers on my desk," she told him.

Larry nodded. "I'll take care of it," he said. I watched as he ran up a nearby staircase, taking two steps at a time.

Stretching out her arms, Mary Jo hugged the disgruntled woman. "God loves you. Your reward will be great in heaven," she told the tanned lady.

Soon Larry appeared. He handed the well-groomed woman a crystal vase filled with roses. "These roses are just for you," Mary Jo told the lady.

Larry leaned over and handed me a small card that he had snatched from the vase of flowers. A day earlier, Mary Jo's daughter had written a sentimental message on the card; it read: "Dear Mom, I love you. Barb."

When Mary Jo rejoined us, she saw that Larry and I were laughing. "That lady needed those roses more than I do. My daughter will understand," Mary Jo said. She began chuckling with us. "God's work should always bring joy."

A few minutes later, Mary Jo and I strolled to the cafeteria. There the usual morning crowd was lining up for the morning meal. I noticed a large man who looked like a professional wrestler; he was pacing past people who were lined up, his vigilant glance sweeping the crowd. Weighing close to 300 pounds, his arms were bulging with muscles, he wore a black T-shirt that read, "Large and In Charge."

"That's Denny," Mary Jo explained. "He lives at Mary's Place with his family. He helps me with security."

With a deep, commanding voice, Denny called the people to attention. "Keep it down. Mary Jo's gonna pray now," he hollered. The obedient crowd grew quiet and still.

Soon Mary Jo began reciting the Lord's Prayer. "Our Father, who art in heaven," she began. Suddenly, I heard two low male voices exchanging angry words. I turned to see a lanky-looking man in an orange tie-dyed shirt pushing Denny. His coarse hair was knotted and his dark eyes looked dazed.

"You can't butt in line!" Denny shouted. The man in the orange shirt whooshed his hand at Denny. "Hey, Fatty, you can't tell me what to do!" the man yelled.

With quick steps, Mary Jo ran towards the arguing men. I was scared. I wanted to shout, "Mary Jo, don't go over there! It's dangerous!"

The man in the orange shirt began arguing with Mary Jo. Finally, like a frustrated mother, she said, "You're just an itsy-bitsy, teeny-weeny, little baby. Why don't you go home and take a nap!"

The lanky man shuffled to a nearby door.

When Mary Jo returned to my side, I was holding my hand over my mouth, trying hard to stifle the urge to chuckle. The incident was over, just like that. Mary Jo had diffused a potentially dangerous situation with a simple scolding.

"God has a good sense of humor. Don't ever forget that," Mary Jo said. She finished reciting the Lord's Prayer. Her cell phone rang from the pocket of her skirt. "I'll be right over," she told the caller.

Walking swiftly, I followed Mary Jo across the street to Mary's Place. "We have a problem. One of the residents, a single mother, she's not keeping her apartment clean," Mary Jo explained. The two of us took an elevator to the second floor. I knew that Mary Jo was a stickler for good house-keeping. "If they don't keep the place clean, they have to leave," Mary Jo said as she pounded on the door of one of the apartments.

A teenage girl opened the door. Wearing a GAP
sweatshirt, her long dark hair was pulled back into a hot
pink hair band. "Mary Jo, it's my mom. Something's wrong,"
the girl cried. The girl led us into the kitchen. There, a
heavyset woman had collapsed on the floor. Wearing a red
blouse that glittered, the large woman was holding her hand
to her chest; her breaths were labored and loud.

"She's having a heart attack," I thought.

The teenage girl began sobbing. "My mom is
hyperventilating. She gets this way when she's stressed. Her
name is Denita," the girl explained between whimpers.

Mary Jo knelt down next to the heavyset woman.
"Denita, we can work with you. Just keep things clean,"
Mary Jo said softly. Gradually, the woman's breaths became
quieter and more rhythmic. The teenage girl stopped crying. I breathed a secret sigh of relief.

"Lets all do some dishes," Mary Jo shouted with glee as
she happily raised her hands toward heaven. For the next
half-hour, we did the dishes. Mary Jo. The teenage girl.
Denita. And me.

While we scrubbed food from pans and wiped down
counters, Mary Jo led us in song: "If you're happy and you
know it, clap your hands...," she sang out, her voice echoing through the apartment.

I couldn't stop grinning. This was God's work. The presence of Christ was here, in this ordinary moment of this
ordinary day at Sharing and Caring Hands. As we stood at
the kitchen sink, doing dishes, we were also exchanging
gifts of laughter and love, powerful gifts that often dissolve
the inevitable conflicts of life. We were celebrating the moment. We were sharing joy. We were rejoicing in the Lord.

For the rest of the morning, I followed Mary Jo as she

ministered to the never-ending needs of the poor. In the midst of all the suffering and pain, Mary Jo continued to smile and laugh and pray. Towards the end of the morning, she even taught me how to do an Irish jig. "Life is a good excuse to dance," she told me.

Later that evening, as the kids and I loaded the dishwasher with the dinner dishes, Christina and Rachael began apologizing for their morning argument. "Mom, we were tired. We stayed up too late the night before," they told me.

"I was crabby, too," I said. I swept the floor while Sarah held the dustpan.

"M-Mom, are you h-happy tonight?" Sarah asked.

In that moment, I felt a fountain of joy welling up inside of me. I was surprised. It was the same kind of joy I had felt on the day I got married, or the afternoon my first book arrived in the mail. Mary Jo had shown me that joy should never be reserved just for special occasions; that true happiness is often hidden in the routine, everyday moments of life.

Rejoice in the Lord always. Now I understood the true meaning of the passage I had pondered that morning. "Sarah, I am happy," I said loudly. I started dancing an Irish jig with my broom.

Christina and Rachael raised their eyebrows as I began tap-dancing. "Oh, no!" they cried out. They buried their faces in their dishtowels. "Mom, you're gone...you've lost it."

Sarah began twirling around the table like a ballerina. "If you're happy and you know it, clap your hands," I sang out. There was love and laughter in my kitchen.

God was here. And that was a reason to rejoice.

SEVEN

Keepin' My Eyes
on da Lord

*"We can experience the peace of heaven by serv-
ing others on earth."*

MARY JO COPELAND

I strolled through a department store with Sarah, the
two of us looking through racks of women's clothing,
all of it marked "clearance." It was Saturday morning.
My family had made arrangements to take me out to dinner
on the following Monday evening. My birthday was coming
up and I needed a new outfit.

"M-Mom, this would l-look pretty on y-you," Sarah said
as she pulled a purple miniskirt from a rack that read "50%
off."

I laughed. "Sarah, I'm in my forties now. I have to wear
sensible things. You try it on," I suggested.

"But Mom, y-you wear too much black and b-black is a
sad color," Sarah said.

My daughter was right. My outdated closet was packed
with black pants and long gray skirts and dark-colored
blouses. Still, I persisted in defending the wardrobe I had

worn for over a decade. "Black is elegant. It goes with everything…it makes me look slim," I said.

Sarah waved a mango-colored dress in front of me. I felt the silkiness of the fabric. The garment was long, and lovely, V-necked with capped sleeves.

"T-try it on. Orange is a h-happy color!" Sarah insisted.

Minutes later, I stood in front of the dressing room mirror, turning to and fro in the bright orange dress. Sarah stood right next to me trying on the purple miniskirt and a trendy top trimmed with silver stars. I helped her zip up the skirt.

"M-Mom, we…look beautiful," she said.

My eyes met hers. She looked so dressed up, so grown up, so much a lady. *Was Sarah really seventeen?* The years had passed so quickly. I could still remember the day she was born, like it was yesterday. "I'm sorry…your daughter has Down's syndrome," the doctor's words rang out from my memory. Though my journey of mothering a handicapped child had been filled with challenge and uncertainty, Sarah's gifts of love and sensitivity had brought purpose and meaning to my life.

Still, as Sarah edged her way towards adulthood, I found myself worrying more and more about her future. Just a week earlier, I had met with Sarah's social worker. "When Sara turns eighteen, there are decisions that must be made," she had said. While handing me forms, the social worker talked of vocational training, group homes, and legal guardianship. I barely listened to her explanations. All I kept thinking was: *Sarah's getting older, and so am I.*

Now, as I studied Sarah's reflection smiling back at me in the dressing room mirror, it hit me. *Sarah is seventeen, but she will always be a child.* I was still taking care of her daily needs, helping her to get dressed, assisting her with meals, and taking her to special education classes and events. *I even tie her shoes.*

Even though my husband helped out as much as possible, taking Sarah to the library and out to breakfast, I was connected to Sarah as only a mother can be. I took care of her when she was sick. I helped her clean her glasses. I washed her hair. At times, I felt like I was a servant.

"You are Sarah's primary caregiver," the social worker had told me time and time again. It was an identity that had remained unchanged since the day of her birth.

I sat down on a bench in the dressing room. I brushed Sarah's face with my hand. "Sarah, purple is your color," I told her. At the same time, I found myself asking the inevitable question that most parents of handicapped children ask: "What will happen to Sarah after I die?"

Throughout the weekend, the question kept echoing through my thoughts. My husband offered a simple solution to Sarah's future. "Honey, don't worry. Things have a way of working out," he said.

Christina and Rachael added their thoughts as well. "Mom, chill out. If something happens to you or Dad, we'll take care of Sarah," they told me. I ignored their words. I envisioned myself getting cancer or multiple sclerosis. I imagined myself dying in a car accident. *Someone has to worry about Sarah.*

Monday morning came. I walked into the crowded cafeteria of Sharing and Caring Hands at 11:00, a little later than usual. I heard Mary Jo's voice make an announcement on the loudspeaker: "Anyone who would like their feet soaked, please join me in the corridor by the sink."

I made my way to a small area near the main office; an informal space lined with blue plastic chairs, wooden cabinets and a large sink. There, Mary Jo was putting on latex gloves while a small bearded man filled up basins of warm, soapy water. He wore a baseball cap that read, "Mystic Lake Casino."

Mary Jo waved to me. "Nancy, do you want to help me wash feet?" she asked. I hesitated. I wasn't sure what she was asking. Drawing nearer, Mary Jo handed me some gloves and a tube of lotion. "It's easy—just follow me," she said.

I shrugged my shoulders. In the past few weeks, I had come to understand that Mary Jo was unlike any other human being I'd ever met. Something unusual, something surprising always happened when I spent time with her.

"I never know what to expect when I come here," I told Mary Jo as I put on the gloves.

She laughed. "Neither do I."

Mary Jo's daily ritual of foot washing began as a few people, mostly men, began taking their places on the folding chairs. While the small gathering began removing their shoes, I couldn't help but notice their feet. Some had swollen toes, scarred with sores and blisters. Others had feet that were red, irritated from walking the streets in worn, wrong-sized shoes. A few even had ulcerated sores with infection setting in.

I watched as the small man in the "casino cap" began placing basins of water at their feet. "Who is he?" I asked. He seemed so efficient. He even put a small kneeling pad on the floor so that Mary Jo could kneel comfortably as she washed feet.

"That's Little Joe. He's an alcoholic. Everyday, he helps me," Mary Jo said softly.

I looked at her curiously. "Does he drink while he's here?" I asked. Mary Jo shook her head. "Never, but I know he drinks at night. Jesus never judged…why should I?" she replied.

With that, Mary Jo knelt in front of a gaunt-looking man dressed in a black T-shirt and jeans embedded with dirt. With his dark hair wild and coiled, he kept rocking back and forth, babbling words and phrases that were hard to understand.

"Hi, Royce. Did you get some breakfast this morning?" she asked. The man kept bobbing. He had a faraway look in his eyes. He smelled like whiskey. Nonetheless, Mary Jo knelt before him, washing his scarred feet. "He has a mental illness. He comes here everyday," she whispered.

I stood by as Mary Jo dried his feet with a towel. She motioned me to squeeze some lotion onto her gloved hand. "Royce, when you get to heaven, what will you say to Jesus?" Mary Jo asked as she rubbed the soothing lotion on his feet. The man continued to speak nonsense. Nonetheless, Mary Jo helped him put on his shoes and tie the laces.

Suddenly, I heard the man speak one sentence, just one, as clear as can be. "Mary Jo been good to me," he said.

Mary Jo moved on to another man who was sitting quietly, soaking his feet. Wearing a striped shirt that was missing two buttons, the man was pale and ill looking. Though he had a rash on his face, and his dark eyes betrayed the yellowish tint of liver problems, he wore a pink-beaded rosary.

"Hello, Anthony, how are you feeling today?" Mary Jo asked as she gently brushed a washcloth over his swollen feet.

"I be keepin' my eyes on da Lord."

I handed Mary Jo a clean towel. The man's eyes met mine. "I got da HIV virus. I ain't got much time," he told me.

Mary Jo dried his feet and helped him put on white socks. "Anthony, when you get to heaven, God will say: 'Well done, good and faithful servant,'" Mary Jo told him.

For a moment, I closed my eyes. Mary Jo talked about heaven in such a matter-of-fact way; she was comfortable with death. She was hopeful, even excited about eternity. *I wish I felt better about dying.*

Mary Jo moved on to a man in his early twenties, a stocky guy with a strong jaw-line and soft brown eyes that betrayed sadness. "My name is Jamalle. I came here from Detroit," he said almost in a whisper. While Mary Jo knelt before him, washing his feet, he winced. "My feet hurt...my shoes don't fit too good," he said. I noticed a pair of dirty tennis shoes propped on a nearby chair with heels worn and full of holes.

Mary Jo tried to change the subject. "Jamalle, it's a beautiful day today. The roses in my backyard are blooming," she told him.

The man's face lit up. "I think roses are God's flower," he said. Mary Jo towel-dried his feet. "Jamalle, what makes you say that?" she asked, her voice filled with a mixture of awe and genuine interest.

Jamalle smiled. "Mary Jo, have you ever smelled anything as sweet as a rose?" he said.

Mary Jo looked as if she was pondering his words. "God made roses with thorns. Sometimes life gives us thorns, doesn't it, Jamalle?" she said.

"Mary Jo, I've made my own thorns...bad decisions... bad relationships...bad everything," he said.

I handed Mary Jo a Band-Aid. I watched as she tenderly affixed it to a sore on the young man's foot. "Jamalle, you have an honest heart. You aren't blaming anyone for your mistakes. God loves you for that," she said.

The man continued to open up to Mary Jo. "I came here to start a new life. I want to get a job at a store…maybe Target or GAP or something like that," he said. Mary Jo called for a volunteer to give him a new pair of shoes. She handed him some bus tokens and three five-dollar bills. She took off her gloves and hugged him. "Take good care of your feet. They must take you a long way in this world, and all the way to heaven," she told him.

The foot-washing ritual came to a close as Mary Jo gathered the poor into a hand-holding circle of prayer. "Lord, bless my friends. Be with them as they journey through this day. Always give them the hope of heaven," she prayed.

After the prayer, as Mary Jo and I washed our hands at the sink, it dawned on me that I had something in common with her. *Mary Jo is a primary caregiver, too.* Each day, she willingly knelt before the children God had given her—the needy, the destitute, the handicapped. She was connected to them as only a mother can be. She assisted them with meals. She comforted them in times of illness. Sometimes she even tied their shoes. Mary Jo was modeling the unconditional love of God, humbly soothing the sores of the poor with the water of mercy and the towel of compassion.

"Mary Jo," I asked as the water from the faucet poured over my hands. "Do you ever worry about what will happen to Sharing and Caring Hands when you're gone?"

Little Joe wove in between us, brushing a cloth over the dust that had collected on Mary Jo's skirt. "I must be a good servant while I can. When the time comes, God will send someone to take my place, maybe even someone better than me," she said.

That evening as I began getting ready to celebrate my birthday, I stood in front of the bathroom mirror putting on makeup. Wearing my new orange dress, Sarah stood right next to me, dressed in her new purple miniskirt. I helped her button up her trendy, star-trimmed top.

"M-Mom...I'm growing up. Can you show me h-how to put on m-makeup?" she asked. She reached into a nearby drawer and pulled out a compact of powder.

"Sure," I said. I showed her how to snap open the compact. "Don't use too much. Smooth it on gently," I told her. While I wisped the rose-colored blush on her cheeks, I recalled the words that Mary Jo had spoken earlier that morning while she washed the feet of the man who was dying of HIV: "When you get to heaven, God will say: 'Well done, good and faithful servant....'"

I felt gratitude for Sarah's presence in my life. Like so many of the poor at Sharing and Caring Hands, she was teaching me how to be a good servant, how to live one day at a time, and how to "keep my eyes on da Lord."

Though my journey of mothering Sarah had been lined with the thorns of uncertainty, the beautiful fragrance of God's presence had remained with me; guiding me, leading me, sustaining me.

I felt strangely reassured about Sarah's future. *I'll be her mother as long as I can. When I'm gone, God will send someone to care for her—maybe even someone better than me.*

It was my birthday. It was a day set aside to celebrate life. It was a day to rejoice in God's ongoing faithfulness. It was a day to replace worry with faith and hope and trust.

"Sarah, we look beautiful, don't we?" I said.

Sarah looked at my dress. "M-Mom," she said. "Orange is such a h-happy color."

Mary Jo speaking to a local church community. Marion Sue Carlin

Mary's Place. Sharing & Caring Hands

Left: *One of the many crosses which decorate the walls of Sharing and Caring Hands.* Marion Sue Carlin

Below: *Mary Jo and Dick Copeland outside their local church in Brooklyn Center, Minnesota.* Marion Sue Carlin

Above: Mary Jo and volunteers stocking the food shelf at Sharing and Caring Hands.

Marion Sue Carlin

Right: One of the hundreds of volunteers who prepare and serve meals each day.

Marion Sue Carlin

Right: *Mary Jo wiping down tables with the assistance of two regular volunteers.*

Marion Sue Carlin

Below: *A large donation area at Sharing and Caring Hands. Here, the needy have daily access to donated clothes, food, and household goods.*

Marion Sue Carlin

Left: *Mary Jo welcoming (then) Governor George Bush to Mary's Place.*
Keri Pickett Photography

Below: *Mary Jo giving Governor George Bush a tour of the Daycare/ Teen Center. Also pictured is Rob Wills, director of the Teen Center.*
Keri Pickett Photography

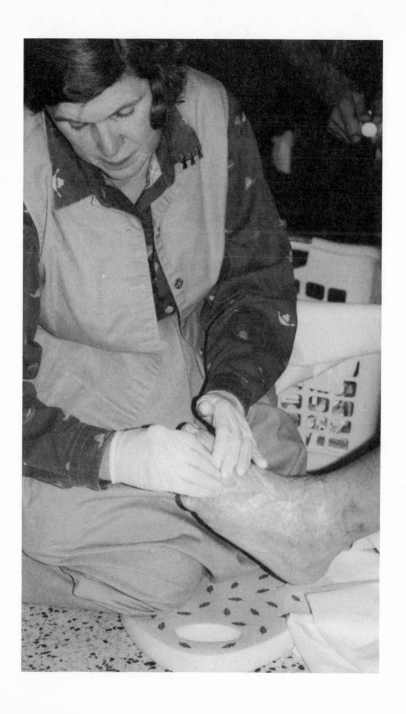

Opposite page: *Mary Jo washing the blistered feet of a homeless man.*

Marion Sue Carlin

This page left:
Foot washing area.

Marion Sue Carlin

This page below:
Mary Jo with one of the regular volunteers.

Marion Sue Carlin

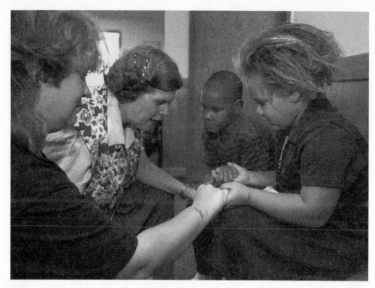

Above: *Mary Jo praying with a family.* Dave Hrbacek

Below: *Two hands clasped in prayer.* Marion Sue Carlin

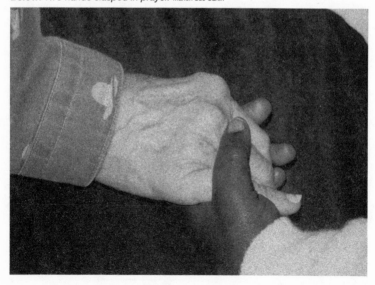

Left: *Mary Jo searching for a child's winter coat, size four.*
Marion Sue Carlin

Below: *"Robbie" Wills, beloved director of the Teen Center.*
Marion Sue Carlin

Mary Jo and "Sarah" sharing a special moment at the Copeland's church in Brooklyn Center, Minnesota. Marion Sue Carlin

EIGHT

God Will See You Through This

"We live in a Good Friday world; and we must
bring the Easter day to everybody we meet."

MARY JO COPELAND

I drove into Sue's driveway and honked the horn. While I waited outside her tidy suburban home, the digital clock on my dashboard clicked to 7:35. That Monday morning, I had made arrangements to meet Mary Jo at Mary's Place, the transitional apartment complex at Sharing and Caring Hands. "I want you to meet my friend," I had told Mary Jo.

From my windshield, I watched as Sue hurried to my van. Tall and pretty with model-like features, Sue wore flowered shorts and an electric blue top. She carried a canvas painting that was almost as tall as she was.

I had known Sue for over twenty years. Once poverty-stricken college roommates, we were now busy mothers with three children apiece. Our enduring friendship was like a cherished quilt.

I popped open the trunk of my minivan. With utmost

care, Sue slid the painting over the back seats. "I want to give this to Mary Jo," Sue said. Like most people in Minneapolis, Sue had learned about Mary Jo's work in newspapers or on television.

I glanced at the work of art, all the while remembering a July morning from the previous summer. In my mind's eye, I saw myself standing in Sue's sunlit dining room, drinking a cup of coffee. Sue was standing in front of a large window, dipping her paintbrush into a pallet of colors on a tray. I watched as she whisked her brush over a life-size canvas that was propped against her table, a painted image of Mary, the Mother of God.

Sue was a natural artist. In college, she had majored in education, placing special emphasis on art and design. In her early twenties, she had worked as an elementary school teacher. A gifted instructor, Sue had taught countless children, including her own, how to sketch and paint and draw.

That morning as I sipped my coffee, Sue blotted earthtone shades over a trailing veil that framed Mary's painted face. "Notice Mary's eyes…she's looking down. She's humble and obedient before God," Sue said.

All I noticed was a black and blue mark on Sue's arm. "Are you okay?" I asked my friend. She just kept stroking her brush over the canvas, adding small details to the praying hands of God's mother. "I'm fine," she said softly.

This wasn't the first time I had seen bruises on Sue. For the last fifteen years, her husband had been abusing her.

I remembered a summer morning years earlier when Sue's children and mine were just toddlers. That morning we were all picnicking at a nearby park. While my three little girls settled into the sand with pails and shovels, Sue lifted her little charges one by one onto nearby swings. Her toddlers squealed with delight as she pushed them three swings at a time.

The two of us shared uproarious laughter as we reminisced about our college days.

"Remember when we were so poor we ate popcorn and lemon drops for a whole week," I shouted from the sand.

Sue giggled. From the swings, she cried out, "Remember our old college house? It sure was a pit, but boy did we have fun."

I glanced her way, my gaze falling on an ugly fist-sized bruise on her upper arm.

"Sue, what happened?" I asked.

"Jake." Her husband's name fell from her mouth like a wounded bird.

My eyes searched her face. "He did this to you?" I was incredulous. "Sue, you don't deserve this. No one does."

Throughout the years of Sue's marriage, there had been emotional bruises as well. Over time, Sue had shared stories of a home life filled with constant criticism and name-calling. On many occasions she had received medical treatment for cuts and bruises. Though I had often encouraged Sue to leave, even providing her with temporary shelter, reasons to stay always emerged from our discussion.

"We're financially secure. My husband is always remorseful. The kids need a father," Sue had said. A spiritual woman, Sue believed that her prayers would bring healing and transformation to her husband. "God can work miracles," she told me as sunlight streamed into her dining room, wrapping her painting in ribbons of light. That morning, I could only pray that God would keep her safe.

The summer memory faded as Sue hopped into the front

seat of my van. In the last few weeks, the violence had esca-
lated in Sue's home. Though Sue knew that it was time to
protect herself and the kids, she lacked the courage to begin
divorce proceedings.

"Sue, I'll help you. You've got to leave," I told her as we
drove down the freeway. She just leaned back in her seat
and sighed. "Despite everything, I still love him," she said.

Minutes later, Sue and I arrived at Mary's Place. After
parking the van, the two of us carried the canvas to a large
social area on the main floor of the complex. Lined with
folding tables and chairs, the spacious room doubled as a
gym, its cement walls trimmed with colorful banners.
Though it was still very early in the morning, a few residents from Mary's Place were already congregating in the
room, mostly mothers and children.

"Mary Jo said she'd meet us here," I told Sue as we leaned
the painting against one of the tables. We smelled Pine-Sol
and heard someone rummaging through an open closet filled
with balls and toys.

"Nancy, you're here…and you brought Sue!" Mary Jo
shouted as she peeked from the closet, waving her dustcloth like a flag.

Mary Jo knew about the ongoing abuse my friend had
suffered. I had told her bits and pieces of Sue's story. During
my weeks at Sharing and Caring Hands, I had seen Mary Jo
help countless women leave violent relationships. Many of
the residents at Mary's Place were single mothers and children trying to rebuild their lives.

"Sue isn't poor, but maybe you can help her," I had told
Mary Jo.

Leaving her dustcloth behind, Mary Jo drew near and
began looking at the painting. Clasping Sue's hand tightly,

Mary Jo took a few quiet moments to study the image of the Blessed Mother.

"Jesus was the center of Mary's life. She trusted him completely and God took care of her," Mary Jo said as she looked knowingly into Sue's eyes.

My friend nodded, absorbing Mary Jo's words like a sponge.

"Sue," Mary Jo continued, "your children need a courageous mother. Trust God, let him give you courage."

Several small children began encircling Mary Jo, clinging to her ankles and reaching for her hands. "Mary Jo! Mary Jo!" they shouted with glee, jumping up and down as they handed her colorful drawings. Mary Jo knelt down and touched the little faces, tenderly. Reaching into her pocket, she handed each child a one-dollar bill. "You can buy an ice cream cone, or some gum," she told them.

Gathering the kids into a circle, Mary Jo began dancing with them, kicking up her heels and skipping. Meanwhile, A maintenance man showed up, a hammer in his hands. He started pounding a large nail into a cement wall that was steps away from our table, the clang of his hammer echoing throughout the room.

While the janitor steadied the painting on the wall, a young mother and her teenage daughter strolled into the social area. They looked like mirrors of one another with identical cheekbones and dark eyes that looked like bright beacons of light.

"I'm Ulanda, and this is my child, Ceil," the mother said.

Sue and I introduced ourselves while the mother and daughter began admiring Sue's colorful reproduction of Mary.

"We ain't Catholic, but Mary Jo told us about God's mom," Ulanda said.

Sue and I listened as Ulanda began sharing a story that sounded painfully familiar. "This past December, I was trying to escape a bad relationship. My husband…he was beatin' me," Ulanda explained.

At that time Ulanda was living in Chicago. A member of a Pentecostal church, Ulanda believed that evil had taken hold of her husband. "I just kept on prayin' for his salvation. I told God I'd stay," Ulanda said.

Some close friends from her church, concerned about Ulanda's safety, told her about Mary Jo. "Go to Minnesota…start a new life. God will save your husband," the friends advised.

Just a day before Christmas, while Ulanda's husband was away, Ulanda and Ceil packed a few belongings in the family car, an old rusted-out station wagon with engine problems. "We left everything behind—our apartment, our friends, even my waitress job," Ulanda told us.

Ulanda and Ceil arrived at Sharing and Caring Hearts on Christmas Eve, late in the afternoon. They were cold and scared and hungry. "It was snowing outside. We had spent all our money on gas. We didn't know anyone in Minneapolis," Ulanda told us.

Ulanda remembered the compassion Mary Jo had shown to her family on that Christmas Eve. "Mary Jo didn't have room for us at Mary's Place, but she put us up in a hotel. She gave us food, some warm coats, and a little money," Ulanda recalled.

Her teenage daughter, Ceil, nodded in agreement. "We live here now. Mary Jo is helping us to start over," Ceil said.

I started remembering the first Christmas. I imagined Mary, the Mother of God, traveling the rough and rocky terrain between Nazareth and Bethlehem. Poor and pregnant, Mary rode uncomfortably on an donkey, not knowing for sure what the future held.

Images of a stable filled my mind, a temporary refuge filled with animals and straw. I could almost see Mary, clad in an earth-tone veil, laying her newborn in a makeshift manger. *Someone helped Mary in her time of need.*

Now tears were welling up in Sue's eyes. She, too, was remembering the first Christmas.

"Ulanda, you were like Mary. Though you were on an uncertain journey, God took care of you," Sue said.

Ulanda seemed to sense that my friend was struggling. "God's gonna take care of you, too," Ulanda said softly.

Taking one last look at the painting, the mother and daughter waved good-bye. It was time for them to eat breakfast. I turned my glance towards the painting. Now, Mary Jo and the children had gathered around the painting; their little eyes glued to the life-size work of art.

"Look at Mary's hands. She's praying to Jesus," Mary Jo told them. The children grew quiet and still. They seemed to sense that there was something special about the portrait. Some of the kids began folding their hands, mimicking the lady in the painting. In those moments of silence, a holiness seemed to cover the social room, like a cozy blanket.

I looked at my friend; her eyes filled with newfound hope and humble resolve. "I can't save my husband, only God can do that," Sue said.

Sue was beginning to see her life in a whole new way. Here, at Mary's Place, truth was taking root in her heart, budding like a rose in a parched desert of doubt and despair. "I need to trust God," she said.

I took her hand. I felt a whole new appreciation for her
friendship and her constant presence in my life. Years earlier, it had been Sue that had helped me through the diffi-
cult months that followed the birth of our Down's syndrome
child. During those uncertain days, Sue called me every day,
just to see how I was doing.

I remembered one afternoon when, as a new mother, I
was battling depression. I'd doubted my ability to raise a
handicapped child. Sue suddenly appeared on my doorstep
holding a pot of homemade vegetable soup and a loaf of
sourdough bread. While the two of us sat at my kitchen
table breaking bread, Sue told me, "God will see you through
this."

Now, many years later, as I clutched Sue's hand, I felt
grateful that I was in the position to return the love and
support that Sue had once given me. It was my turn to extend my sharing and caring hands; and I welcomed the opportunity.

Still surrounded by the children, Mary Jo turned her
glance to our table, the colorful painting, now a beautiful
backdrop of color on a gray cement wall.

"Sue, God loves you. He will give you strength for
the journey!" Mary Jo shouted. Her comforting words
echoed across the gym like a mighty message from heaven.

The following week, Sue secured a restraining order on
her husband. She saw a lawyer and began proceedings for a
divorce. She made counseling appointments for herself and
for each of her children. She even made plans to return to
work.

Throughout the week, I talked with Sue on the phone—
almost every day—just to see how she was doing. One afternoon, she called me, her voice filled with anxiety.

"I don't know what the future holds," she told me. A few hours later, I showed up on her doorstep, holding a pot of homemade vegetable soup and a loaf of sourdough bread. As we sat at the kitchen table breaking bread, I felt the unmistakable presence of God.

"Sue," I said, "God will see you through this."

Sharing and Caring Hands was in my midst.

NINE

True Love

"Don't pray too long, you'll get it wrong; we
must go from prayer to action."
MARY JO COPELAND

M y kitchen table was covered with our monthly
bills. Sarah read an illustrated Cinderella book
while I wrote out checks to the garbage man, the
mortgage company, and assorted doctors and dentists. That
Thursday evening, the rest of the family had gone to watch
Rachael's soccer game. I was glad that Sarah had stayed behind. It was good to have company while I completed the
household task I dreaded most.

While I sealed envelopes, Sarah guided her finger over
the pages of her book, carefully following each letter and
sentence. Cinderella was Sarah's favorite fairy tale. She read
it cover to cover, almost every night. Though she couldn't
pronounce every word, she had memorized certain phrases.

"Cinderella was…was p-poor. She s-sat in the ashes.
Nobody loved h-her," my daughter read as I stacked the
ready-to-mail bills in a pile.

Turning to the last page of her story, Sarah sighed long-
ingly. "M-Mom, Cinderella found t-true love," she mused.

With a dreamy look in her eyes, she pointed to a colorful picture of Cinderella, dressed in a long white gown, a crown on her head and ruby jewels around her neck.

I took a peek at the picture. With a wealthy looking prince at her side, Cinderella was surrounded by a crowd of regally robed relatives, all of them beaming as they welcomed the former peasant-girl into their royal clan.

"Cinderella got rich, too," I said jokingly as I looked at the stately castle that gleamed in the background of the picture.

I thought about an old college acquaintance who was now a successful lawyer. The mother of three children, she was married to a doctor and lived in an expensive Colonial home that overlooked a prestigious lake. Along with a personal trainer that visited her each week, she had a live-in nanny for her kids and a chef who prepared her evening meals.

"Sarah, wouldn't it be nice to be rich?" I asked. Resting my chin on one hand, I gazed at the pillars and water fountains and gold streets that trimmed Cinderella's royal mansion. I thought about our family finances.

As a freelance writer, my salary was completely dependent on unpredictable royalties and advances. Though my husband's teaching job brought in a regular income, we often had to juggle our family budget to make ends meet. Oftentimes, when the kids asked to go to the mall or to the movies, I would say, "You'll have to wait until I get paid."

Though my family supported me in my writing career, sometimes I wondered if I should get a "real job." I imagined myself working a nine-to-five job in an office or a large corporation. I thought about TV commercials I had seen while watching the six o'clock news; ads that proclaimed the importance of stocks and bonds and "building a financial portfolio."

I could only imagine what it would be like to have an authentic "financial portfolio." Our family lived check to check. "We're making it," I whispered, assuring myself that we had a little money in savings, a little money in retirement, and a little money set aside for the kids' college. Still, I wondered what would happen if my husband lost his job or I lost my income.

Sarah nudged my arm. "Mom, if you were Cinderella, w-what would your castle look like?" she asked. I got a faraway look in my eyes, glad that she had asked. I had often imagined the house of my dreams.

"Sarah, my castle would be on the water, a little Cape Cod with a wraparound porch," I said. I began describing an oceanfront property I had once seen on the Home and Garden channel. "I'd have wicker furniture and stained-glass lamps and floral couches," I told her.

Sarah giggled as she made her way to the refrigerator and retrieved two cans of soda. "Mom, let's...let's...have a toast," she said as she handed me a can of Dr. Pepper.

Sarah often led our family in "kitchen-table toasts" whenever we gathered for dinner or birthday parties.

"To castles...," she said, her eyes twinkling as she raised her can of cola.

I clicked my can to hers, a grin on my face. "To castles...," I replied.

Monday morning came. When I walked into the cafeteria of Sharing and Caring Hands, I saw the usual line of people crowding around Mary Jo. I watched as volunteers rushed to and fro, following Mary Jo's tender directives to fetch shoes or food or cash for those she deemed needy.

"Nancy," Mary Jo called out from the crowd that hemmed her in. Weaving my way to the front of the line, Mary Jo handed me a pad of paper and a ballpoint pen. "It's crazy this morning. I need your help. Will you do some interviews for me?" Mary Jo asked.

While the line continued to grow, Mary Jo explained that each day, her ministry collected Social Security numbers on all those who received assistance. "Go through the line; talk with each person. Get their story and their Social Security number," Mary Jo instructed as she took a moment to kneel down and brush the face of a small boy.

"What do I do then?" I asked as Mary Jo moved on to the next person in line, a curly-haired woman wearing glasses that were too big for her face.

"Just tell me what you find out. I'll decide who needs help," she said.

With pen in hand, I sat down at a nearby table and noticed a mother in her late thirties, encircled by three children, all of them preteen. I nodded, encouraging them to join me at the table.

They quietly took their places around me, leaning their rolling suitcases against the table. I wondered why they had come to Sharing and Caring Hands. They were all well groomed and stylishly dressed. Wearing a crisp white button-down blouse, the mother's blonde hair was cut into a classy style, her nails long and polished. Her kids, also blonde and freckled, wore clean, fashionable clothes that looked like they came from J.Crew.

"My name is Karla…this is so hard for me," the mother admitted, her face flushed with embarrassment.

"It's okay. I just need to get a bit of information," I replied, trying to sound as respectful as I could. I listened as Karla began telling me why she was there.

"Up until three weeks ago, we had a house in Burnsville," she said. I nodded. Burnsville was a lovely middle- to upper-class neighborhood known for its tree-lined streets and tidy homes. Karla explained that her husband had lost his job a few months earlier. "He went into a depression. He just...left us," she said.

Teary-eyed, Karla went on to say that she had always been a stay-at-home mom. "We were financially secure. We had some money in savings, but it only took five months for us to lose our home," she said.

Mary Jo drew near to our table, bending her ear as I quietly relayed their story.

"Oh," Mary Jo shouted with childlike glee as she took Karla's hand. "I have an apartment for you. It's safe, it has everything you need, a TV, a nice clean kitchen, and beds for the kids." Mary Jo reached into her skirt pocket and handed Karla $75 for food. "Everything will be okay, you'll see," Mary Jo said as she merrily clapped her hands.

"Soon, you'll find a little job. Soon, you'll find another home. Soon, you'll have enough pocket change to go to Dairy Queen every Friday night," Mary Jo said with a laugh.

The kids giggled as Mary Jo gathered the family, and me, into a circle of prayer. "Lord, bless my friends. You love them and so do I," she prayed.

In turn, a volunteer appeared to escort Karla and her kids to their temporary apartment.

"Mary Jo," I said softly, my voice betraying dismay. "Karla was from the suburbs. If she can lose their home, so can I," I told her.

Mary Jo whooshed her hand at me, as if I was wasting time on worry. "Come back on Thursday afternoon. I have to run a support meeting. You'll feel better if you come," she said.

The following Wednesday, at 4:15 in the afternoon, I walked into a large meeting room at Mary's Place. I saw five rows of folding chairs arranged in a semicircle, most of the chairs occupied by residents of the apartments, all of them waiting for Mary Jo to arrive.

Taking an empty place in the front row, I sat next to an elderly man with a walker. While people talked quietly, I heard the sounds of a small baby, cooing. I turned around and saw a boyish looking man, wearing a baseball cap turned backwards, rocking a newborn in his arms. I smiled at him. He nodded politely.

Moments later, Mary Jo arrived as everyone applauded. Waving and smiling, she walked to the front of the room like she was a popular politician about to give a rousing speech.

"Dear friends," she began, her face radiant. "This afternoon, I'd like to begin with a story." Wearing a khaki skirt and matching vest, Mary Jo began remembering the years when she was a stay-at-home mom raising twelve children. "There was always wash piled in my laundry room. One afternoon, the washing machine broke down. I just sat on the front steps and buried my head in my hands," she recalled. Mary Jo told the gathering how helpless she had felt on that afternoon. "I cried a little bit, I prayed a little bit, and then I asked God to help me."

Minutes later, the Maytag repairman arrived at her door. "He saw me crying on the front steps. He told me things would get better...then he fixed my machine." Mary Jo's eyes scanned the audience. "Things will get better for you, too," she said with a loud clap of her hands. "God will help you fix your life," she added.

Cheers erupted as Mary Jo continued to preach words of inspiration. "Maybe you're feeling sorry for yourself. Maybe you've lost your home, your car, your job, your health...," she said.

I looked around. Everyone was sitting on the edge of their chairs, nodding, their eyes glued on Mary Jo. They almost looked like they were watching a suspense thriller on a wide-screen TV.

I listened in awe as Mary Jo admonished them to stop complaining and start trusting God. "If you're an addict, get into treatment. If you don't have a job, go get one. If you're sick or handicapped, let God help you...let me help you," she said. Then raising her hands she declared, "Only God can bring true security to our lives."

Voices rang out from different parts of the room. "Amen! Alleluia! Thank you, Jesus!" came the joyful cries. Suddenly Mary Jo's prayer meeting took on the appearance of a lively Pentecostal worship service. People were hugging each other and bowing their heads in silent prayer.

"Mary Jo, you helped me when the rest of the world turned their back on me!" the boyish looking father in the row behind me called out.

"I think ya all are a saint," said a large woman with a flowered scarf on her head.

The elderly man with the walker took a handkerchief from his pocket and began wiping away tears.

"Here's the bottom line," Mary Jo said, her eyes filling with twinkling wisdom. "You are responsible for the effort. God will take care of the outcome," she declared. She told them that life was a gift that deserved to be celebrated. "I have three words of advice for you," Mary Jo declared. "Don't pray too long, you'll get it wrong; we must go from prayer to action."

I was moved; deeply moved. Most of the people in that room had no savings or stocks or bonds, yet God had blessed them with untold riches of unshakable faith and undying hope. Though the poor that surrounded me had no financial portfolio, they had something better, something even more secure. It was true love. God's love. Mary Jo's love. Each other's love.

In an instant, I no longer felt fearful about our family's financial future. *If we lose our jobs, we'll find other ones. If we lose our house, we'll find another place to live. Whatever happens, God will help fix our lives.*

Just before Mary Jo closed the meeting with a prayer, she swooped her hands towards my front row chair. "This is Nancy…she's writing a book about trusting God!" Mary Jo declared. Again, voices rang out from all parts of the room, "Amen, sister! God be praised! Bless you, honey!" came the unexpected calls of support.

The man sitting next to me saw me wiping away a tear. He patted my arm. "It's okay…Mary Jo makes us all cry," he said.

Mary Jo reached into her pocket and brought me a Kleenex. Though I was sitting in the front row, my emotions on display, I felt no shame.

Just weeks earlier, I had accepted Mary Jo's invitation to write a book about the poor. Originally, I had thought I would write a heartwarming story, something that would help the world to understand the hardships of living in poverty. Now I was beginning to understand that homelessness was a blessing, albeit a strange one. *When people have nothing, they let God love them.*

Later that evening, when I arrived home, I saw Sarah sitting at the kitchen table, once more reading her cherished Cinderella book.

"Mom...Cinderella l-lived h-happily ever after," Sarah said as she looked up from her book, her thick glasses framing her almond shaped eyes.

I sat down beside her, gazing at the same illustration that I had studied just days earlier. Now I hardly noticed the stately castle that trimmed the colorful illustration. It was Cinderella's face that drew me in: she was beaming, smiling, rejoicing. Though she had once lived a life of poverty, covered with the ashes of loneliness and despair, now she had the love and support of a brand new family.

I felt a new appreciation for my husband and kids. Though we weren't rich, and we didn't live in a castle, God's true love was with us. It was this unchanging love and faithfulness that made our family secure. Every part of our lives was in his hands, even our finances, both present and future. He would take care of us, no matter what the future held.

"Sarah, let's have a toast," I said as I pulled two crystal goblets from a nearby hutch. After pouring red Kool-Aid into the glasses, I handed Sarah her cup.

"M-Mom...what...s-should we...we toast?" Sarah asked excitedly. I could tell she welcomed my impromptu invitation to celebrate life.

"How about love?" I said, as I raised my glass, waving it playfully.

Sarah clicked her cup to mine. She laughed. She thought I was joking, but she played right along. "To love," she said, "t-true...true love."

TEN

Halos, Harps, and Hope

"We are all called to be channels of God's peace, instruments of His love."

MARY JO COPELAND

Christina's room smelled like fresh paint as we moved her bed and furniture into place. We had spent most of the weekend, Christina and I, painting her bedroom "Trail Pink," a tropical shade that looked like fuchsia.

With dried paint still splattered on our hands, the two of us began reorganizing her room. While I hung new white lace on her windows, Christina pinned posters and pictures on her walls.

"Mom, where should I put these?" Christina asked as she began unpacking a set of ceramic angels from a cardboard box.

I waved my hand, proudly, towards a shelf that I had just rehung. One by one, Christina placed each winged keepsake, carefully, on the shelf. There were fifteen cherubs in all; she cherished the collection. Throughout her life, I had given her one angel, each year, on her birthday.

"Yesssssssss," Christina said as she added the last angel

to the sentimental display. Exhausted, the two of us sat down on her bed, quietly admiring the dramatic transformation of her teenage retreat. It had been a good weekend. While rolling paint and taping trim, we had covered an array of adolescent topics—school, sports, and friends. We had even come up with a profile for the perfect boyfriend: "Cute...smart...kind...," Christina had said.

Now, as we sat on her bed, it dawned on me that Christina would be going off to college in three years. *She's growing up too fast.* I found myself wishing that she would always be fifteen, that she would never move away, that she would always live in this two-story house, right here in this room we had just painted pink.

Just then, we heard the sound of a loud crash, glass shattering. "Mom, my angels!" Christina cried out, one hand over her mouth. The shelf I had just hung was now lying on the floor, the brackets improperly secured.

"Oh, Christina," I gasped. Broken pieces of halos and harps were scattered on the floor, some in shards. In a moment, Christina's prize collection was nothing more than a painful mosaic of fragmented glass.

"Mom, why did it have to happen? Why?" Christina pleaded as she cradled a broken wing in her hand. She started crying, softly, her tears dropping to the floor. In silence, I began helping her pick up the pieces, not knowing how to comfort her. I knew that my daughter wasn't just crying over her angels; there were other broken things in her life.

Over the weekend, Christina had opened up to me, sharing long-buried feelings about her handicapped sister. "Mom, I hate it when people stare at Sarah," Christina had said. While the two of us slid paintbrushes around her windows,

Christina recalled a recent shopping trip our family had taken to the mall.

On that afternoon, while I helped Rachael try on jeans in a large department store, I asked Christina to keep an eye on Sarah. Just for fun, Christina had taken Sarah to the accessories department where hats were displayed. While the two of them stood in front of a large mirror, trying on flowered head scarves, three teenage girls, all of them tall and pretty, approached them.

"Mom, they pointed at us...they laughed at us. They called Sarah a retard," Christina remembered as she painted the trim around her closet.

As our weekend of painting wore on, Christina recalled similar stories; her bottled up feelings flowing like an unstoppable waterfall.

"Mom, I love Sarah. But why was she born handicapped? Why did it have to happen?" she said, all the while waving her paintbrush in frustration.

Now, Christina's questions echoed through my mind as I helped my daughter sift through the larger, salvageable pieces of her broken angels.

Years earlier, I had asked those same questions. I thought back to the first months of Sarah's life. "Why, God? Why did this happen?" I often cried out as I cradled my Down's syndrome baby in my arms.

As a new mother, I was angry at God. Sarah's handicap was permanent, her genes and chromosomes unalterable. No amount of prayer would take away her disability. There would be no closure to her handicap; no miraculous healing would come. Sarah would always have slanted eyes and low muscle tone and limited intellect. And I would always be her mother.

As the years passed and Sarah grew, I began to see that her disability was drawing me closer to God. Sarah, even with all her delays and imperfections, was teaching me how to live with the questions, to learn from them, even to rejoice in them. She was helping me to understand that the "why's" of her existence were the very things that were making me better, stronger, wiser.

"Christina, there's some glue downstairs...we can fix these," I told my daughter as we placed shattered ceramic faces and feet into a box.

"They'll always be broken," Christian said as she buried her face in my shoulder.

I couldn't fix the angels anymore than I could fix Christina's feelings about her disabled sister. In that moment, I wanted to tell Christina, "Wait and see...the imperfections of Sarah's life will make you a better person...she will lead you to God," but I didn't. These were spiritual lessons that she would need to learn on her own. It was all part of growing up.

"Just cry," I told her.

The next morning, before I left for Sharing and Caring Hands, I ate a quick breakfast with Christina and Sarah at the kitchen table.

With Rachael at summer soccer and Don already at work, it was just the three of us. Christina munched on a bowl of Cap'n Crunch. I looked across the table and said, "I'm going to meet Mary Jo at the teen center. Sarah's coming with me...why don't you come?"

At first, Christina shook her head. I could tell that the sadness of the previous night still lingered.

"Christina...it w-will be f-fun...c-come," Sarah pleaded.

I kept insisting, reminding Christina how bored she had

been on summer vacation. "It'll be an adventure," I told my daughter.

Forty-five minutes later, Christina, Sarah, and myself arrived at Mary's Hope, the teen center at Sharing and Caring Hands. Once an old storefront, the center was now a safe gathering place for the homeless teens who lived in the adjacent housing complex.

When we walked into the center, we found ourselves standing in a large room that was furnished with plaid couches and pool tables. There was a weight training room and a long table where video games flashed on several television screens. It was noisy. Rap music was playing in the background. Three teenage girls dressed in low riding jeans and tank tops danced, waving to us as we passed by. There were kids everywhere, talking, laughing, holding pool cues, soda cans, and remote controls.

"Mom, look," Christina said as she pointed to a mural on the wall. It read: "Your life is God's gift to you…what you do with your life is your gift to God."

Soon a fit looking man wearing a visored "Chicago Cubs" cap drew near, his massive arms steering his wheelchair, effortlessly, to our side.

"I'm Robbie. I run this place. Mary Jo is running late," he said, his voice husky.

I guessed that Robbie was in his mid-thirties, though his handsome face, thick-necked and strong-boned, had the look of a hunky high school athlete.

"Let me show you around," he said as he steered his chair towards the weight area.

My daughters and I watched as Robbie showed an overweight boy how to lift 100 pounds of barbells. "Arms straight…lift with your shoulders. Do ten in a row," Robbie coached. While Robbie counted the boy's lifts, a younger child, a boy about twelve, snuck up behind his wheelchair. He put his small hands over Robbie's eyes.

"Gotcha!" Robbie shouted. Christina and Sarah laughed as Robbie locked his mighty arm around the boy's neck, gripping the unsuspecting child in an immovable headlock.

"You're good at what you do," I told Robbie as I sat down with my daughters on a nearby bench.

"Most of the kids here don't have a father figure. I think they trust me, with the wheelchair and all," Robbie explained.

While Robbie tried to carry on a conversation with us, the teenage kids kept drawing near to his wheelchair. They leaned on him. They ruffled his hair. They hugged him. One boy with a pierced nose engaged Robbie in a playful punching match. "You're a wimp," Robbie told him with a laugh.

"How did you get this job?" I asked Robbie as a young girl, about sixteen, sat down right next to Christina. Wearing colorful beads in her dark-braided hair, the girl wore thick eyeliner and heavy lip gloss. It was obvious she was curious about who we were and what we were talking about.

"I grew up a few blocks away from Mary Jo. I used to call her Mrs. Copeland," Robbie said as he reminisced about his boyhood days. "When I was nineteen, I got into a car accident. The doctors told me I'd never walk, never play sports, never get married," Robbie remembered.

The girl wearing makeup listened intently, her eyes wide. Christina nodded as Robbie continued with his story. Sarah just swung her legs and smiled.

"After the accident, I went into a slump...you know, an

emotional crisis. I kept asking God, 'Why me?'" Robbie remembered the day Mary Jo called him and asked if he wanted a job.

"She told me that God had a plan for my life, that I was the one who was supposed to run the teen center. I've been here ever since," Robbie said.

Robbie went on to say that he was now a professional weightlifter, that he owned his own home and that he had countless friends who enriched his life. "The accident was hard, but it made me a stronger person. Now, my life has meaning. Every morning, I pray that these kids will see God in me," he said.

Just then, one of the kids cranked up the rap music full blast, a loud, rhythmic drumbeat resonating throughout the room. "I'll be right back," Robbie said.

While Robbie wheeled his chair away, the girl wearing makeup eyed Sarah, her scrutinizing glance obvious.

"What's your name?" I asked the girl, trying to distract her from looking at Sarah.

"Nateesha," the girl replied. Christina squirmed, uncomfortable at the girl's stare.

"How old is she?" Nateesha asked, pointing to Sarah.

"She's seventeen," Christina said curtly, certain that Nateesha was about to make fun of Sarah's appearance.

"I got a sister…she's nine. She can't talk or walk or eat by herself. The doctors said she got somethin' called spina bifida," Nateesha explained.

Tears welled up in Nateesha's eyes, her eyeliner melting on her face. "People make fun of her…my mama says my sister is gonna make me into a…you know…sensitive person, but it's hard," Nateesha said, her eyes now locking with Christina's.

"Listen up!" Robbie yelled. "Mary Jo is here. She wants to talk to all you guys. Let's gather in a circle," he shouted. I turned to find Mary Jo standing by Robbie's side, waving, smiling, and beckoning the kids to join her by the pool table. In an instant, a hush fell over the teen center. The video games were all turned off. Soda cans were discarded and pool cues were set aside.

From all corners of the room, the teenage kids encircled Mary Jo's folding chair; they looked like expectant children, waiting to hear a good story. While Robbie and I sat next to Mary Jo, Christina, Sarah, and Nateesha sat side by side, cross-legged on the floor.

"How are you doing today?" Mary Jo asked, as her eyes, filled with compassion, scanned each teenage face. "You know, people on the outside might think you're homeless, but you aren't homeless, really," Mary Jo began. She told the kids that the "Light of Love" was always shining for them. "You are welcome here; this is your home. God loves you, and so do I," Mary Jo said.

A broad-shouldered boy wearing baggy pants and a lime-green T-shirt was the first to speak. "Mary Jo...it's safe here. Not like out on the streets," he said.

A freckled girl with Irish red hair added her candid thoughts. "A few months ago, my dad left us...my mom was so sad. She didn't think life was worth living. Mary Jo, you saved our lives," the girl said.

Nateesha nodded. "Everyone here is accepted. Every-one!" she said, her glance turning to Sarah.

While Mary Jo went around the room checking in with each teen, Christina absorbed every word that was spoken.

"I know how God operates," Mary Jo said. "He always brings something good out of pain. Your life may be hard right now but just wait a few years. You'll see. God will use your suffering to help the world," she said.

When the meeting came to a close, Mary Jo raised her hands high and said, "Let's have a prayer."

Christina, Sarah, and Nateesha linked hands while the other teens followed their lead, their circle of prayer an unbreakable chain of love.

"Lord, bless these special servants. Use their hardships to make them holy," Mary Jo prayed.

Later that evening, Christina and I found ourselves sitting on the floor of her newly painted room. While I spread Super glue over the edges of broken angel parts, Christina began piecing together her ceramic keepsakes.

"Mom...today, when were at the teen center...no one made fun of Sarah," she said as she glued together two ceramic wings. "That's the only place in the whole wide world where everyone accepted her. God was there...I know he was," she added.

I was proud of her. Christina was growing up. She was beginning to understand that Sarah's life, imperfect as it was, was increasing her faith and making her better, stronger, wiser. Mary Jo and Robbie and Nateesha had shown Christina that the "why's" of life draw us ever closer to God and connect us to one another in beautiful, unbreakable bonds.

Sarah peeked into Christina's room, watching as her sister placed each glue-globbed angel on the shelf.

"C-Christina...your...your angels...t-they l-look funny," Sarah said, as she pointed to a headless cherub.

Christina started giggling, her shoulders shaking. "Sarah, work with me here...I'm trying to fix 'em," Christina said. There wasn't a trace of sadness or remorse in Christina's voice.

I looked at the shelf where fifteen mended angels were now displayed; some were wingless, others were missing a hand or a harp. All of the ceramic treasures were leaning a little to the right. I couldn't help it; I started laughing, too.

"They do look a little funny," I said, trying not to laugh too hard.

In an instant, the three of us flopped on Christina's bed, doubling over with laughter, holding our stomachs.

We were rejoicing, triumphing over the brokenness of our lives. The mended angels would forever remind Christina, and me, that imperfection is a blessing in disguise.

God was present in Christina's Trail-Pink room.

ELEVEN

Yes

"What is God calling you to do? Maybe he's calling you to get out of an unhealthy relationship. Maybe he's calling you to visit a nursing home. Maybe he's calling you to smile. Maybe he's calling you to give someone a rose."

MARY JO COPELAND

The digital clock on my home computer read 1:05 A.M. With the book manuscript due in just a few days, I was working day and night to meet the publishing deadline. Unedited chapters now covered my desk; I scrambled to correct misspelled words and rewrite poorly structured sentences.

I reached for my cup of coffee, my glasses falling down over my nose. The house was quiet, my family upstairs, fast asleep. I fought to keep my eyes open. "That's it. I'm done for tonight," I said as I clicked off my computer.

Drawing near to the living room window, I pulled open the drapes. A warm summer breeze blew through the open screen. I could hear crickets chirping and the lull of a plane flying above. Our front yard was dark, all except for the lamppost by the driveway, its light shining.

From my window, I could see the garden that encircled the outdoor lamp. Yellow pansies and tall scarlet roses bloomed in the night. It was a beautiful sight to behold. The reflection from the lamppost formed the shape of a shimmering star, illuminating the colorful blooms.

I heard the sound of soft slippered footsteps coming down the stairs.

"M-M-Mom...w-why are you awake?" a small voice stuttered from the landing. I turned to find Sarah, her curly hair pulled back into a yellow scrunchy, her long nightgown patterned with prints of Cinderella.

I motioned her near. For a moment, the two of us stood together, wrapped in silence that felt sacred. "Sarah, tomorrow is my last day with Mary Jo. I'm a little sad," I told her.

"Hmmmm," Sarah said as she brushed her hand over her chin like a wise sage. "W-why are you s-sad? You found God...didn't y-you?" she asked.

I sighed. Just a few weeks earlier, on a cold winter night, Sarah and I had stood at this very window, the outdoor lamppost veiled in blowing snow. On that chilly night, my heart was searching for God, longing to know, to feel, the light of his presence in my busy life.

I began remembering the first Monday I had spent with Mary Jo Copeland. On that snow-flecked morning, I had arrived on the doorstep of Sharing and Caring Hands, like so many of the needy people in downtown Minneapolis.

I had come to Mary Jo "poor in spirit," worn and tired from the daily demands of my life. Mary Jo had extended her caring hands to me, a stranger in her midst, an everyday person shivering in the whirlwinds of responsibilities and commitments; an ordinary mother, hungry, starving for meaning in her life.

My ten Mondays at Sharing and Caring Hands had been much more than a writing project; it had been a retreat, a spiritual classroom, an undeserved gift of love from God. Mary Jo and the poor had shown me that God's presence can never be limited to a chapel or a hospital room or a devotional book filled with uplifting quotes and prayers. I now knew that God could be found in the ordinariness of my life, in everyday places and faces; in my kitchen, my minivan, my children's rooms.

Sarah pointed to the light in our front yard. "M-Mom, it's so b-bright," she said. I looked at the sparkling lamp-post. In my mind, I went over my new spiritual checklist for living:

Rejoice always,
Pray constantly,
Be a good servant.

From the panes of my living room, I marveled at the scarlet rose bushes, their brightly lit blossoms concealing thorny branches. I could almost hear Sister Claire calling out from my second-grade memory: "The beauty of God's love will always overshadow the thorns of our lives."

I continued my mental checklist:

Don't fear…
Don't fear finances…
or death…
or brokenness…
or the future…
God is in control of all these things.

Sarah laid her head on my shoulder. I felt God's peace, hovering. There had never been a need to search for God. He had always been right here, in my home, my heart, waiting for me to recognize him.

"Sarah, I think God found me," I said softly.

The next morning, I arrived at Sharing and Caring Hands carrying a small gift for Mary Jo. With the floral-wrapped present in my hand, I walked through the cafeteria where the poor sat at tables, eating scrambled eggs and toast. After spending so many weeks at Sharing and Caring Hands, I now recognized faces. Many of the poor waved and smiled at me as I passed by. I waved back.

Mary Jo was washing feet nearby. I drew near just as Little Joe placed a basin of water before a large man who clutched a dirty backpack on his lap. He was crying. Mary Jo didn't notice me right away; she was busy, kneeling before the man, helping him to take off his dusty, hole-dotted boots.

I sat down in a nearby chair. The man was probably in his mid forties. He was unshaven, bags under his puffy, tear-filled eyes.

"M-M-Mary Jo, I…I…I walked 300 miles…from Blue Earth R-Reservation," the crying man stuttered. I looked at his feet; there were large blisters on his toes. His ankles were red and swollen. He looked like a lost puppy; his dark eyes hollow and afraid. With his clothes still wet from the rain outside, he was shivering.

The man was handicapped. I knew it, intuitively. In so many ways, he reminded me of Sarah.

Still kneeling before him, Mary Jo reached into her skirt pocket and pulled out a Kleenex. She dried his tears, looking into his face, tenderly.

"What's your name?" she asked the man. Mary Jo kept looking into his eyes.

"Melvin…," the man replied, whimpering.

"That's a nice name…it's strong…Melvin…," Mary Jo told him.

Soon a male volunteer appeared. He handed Mary Jo clean white socks and a pair of large-sized men's shoes.

"Take this man to Target. He needs some new clothes," Mary Jo told the volunteer. "Call the Salvation Army, he needs a room; get him some food, he's hungry," Mary Jo declared.

The man kept crying, his tears streaming down his face and dropping into the basin below. Several other street people began encircling him, protectively.

I looked at the holes in his boots. It was clear that he had traveled many miles, most likely alone. I was sure that his path had been strewn with the rocks of loneliness and the thorns of darkness and despair.

On his journey, he had probably been searching for the things we all seek in life: hope, compassion, true love.

Like so many others, his journey had brought him to Sharing and Caring Hands, to this safe, holy haven that looked and felt a lot like heaven.

Here, at this very unconventional church, Melvin had found God in Mary Jo Copeland. She was a blooming rose on his pathway of pain, a shining lamppost on his road of rain.

So, too, Mary Jo had found God in this dirty, tattered traveler that was now soaking his wounded feet. On this ordinary day at Sharing and Caring Hands, Mary Jo was caring for the "flock" that God had given her. I knew that her acts of kindness held eternal significance. In drying Melvin's tears, Mary Jo was really drying the tears of Christ.

A passage from the Gospel of Matthew surfaced in my memory as I recalled the words of Jesus: "I was hungry and you gave me food, I was thirsty and you gave me something to drink, I was a stranger and you welcomed me, I was naked and you gave me clothing, I was sick and you took care of me, I was in prison and you visited me…just as you did it to one of the least of these who are members of my family, you did it to me" (25:34–40).

When Mary Jo handed Melvin some bus tokens and three ten-dollar bills, I looked at my watch. With my deadline looming, it was time to get back to work. It was time to return to my busy life. It was time to say yes to all that God had asked me to do.

> *I needed to write for God.*
> *I needed to clean my house for God.*
> *I needed to love, just love, all the people God had*
>   *placed on my daily path: my family, my friends,*
>   *and of course, the needy strangers that I might*
>   *happen to meet on my journey.*

"Mary Jo," I called out from my chair. "I brought you a gift. I'll leave it by your office."

Still kneeling before Melvin, Mary Jo's eyes met mine. She grinned at me. Though her hand was covered with a latex glove, she waved good-bye. "Nancy, God loves you and so do I!" she shouted.

I felt a lump in my throat. Though I knew I would return to Sharing and Caring Hands as a volunteer, I would miss the special time I had spent with Mary Jo. I would never forget all the "Melvins" that I had come to know; I would always remember the lessons I had learned.

"I love you, too," I told Mary Jo. Like me, Mary Jo was busy with the work God had given her to do. Sharing and Caring Hands was her "yes" to God.

Making my way towards her office, I placed the floral-wrapped present at her doorway. Taking a small card from my purse, I scribbled a few words: "Mary Jo, may grace and peace be yours in abundance," I wrote. I tucked the card under a lacy bow, then turned and walked away, smiling.

Beneath the floral wrapping was a framed print...a picture of a rose.

Lo, How a Rose E'er Blooming

Lo, how a Rose e'er blooming from tender stem
    hath sprung!
Of Jesse's lineage coming, as those of old
    have sung.
It came, a floweret bright, amid the cold of
    winter, when half spent was the night.

Isaiah 'twas fortold it, the Rose I have in mind;
with Mary we behold it, the Virgin Mother kind.
To show God's love aright, she bore to us a Savior,
when half spent was the night.

O Flower, whose fragrance tender with
    sweetness fills the air,
dispel in glorious splendor the darkness
    everywhere.
True man yet very God, from sin and death now
    save us, and share our every load.

Words, st. 1–2, 15th Century German, trans. by Theodore Baker 1894, st. 3 from The Hymnal, 1940 (Isa 35:1–2). St. 3, Friedrich Layritz; tr. Harriet Reynolds Krauth Spaeth; ver. Hymnal 1940, © Church Pension Fund, used by permission.

Wisdom for the Journey

Quotes From Mary Jo Copeland

- Love and Compassion are the secret to world peace.

- People are starved for love. Everyday, when I meet the poor, I hug them and they don't want to let me go. I always ask myself, "How long has it been since one of these dear ones has been touched?"

- What is success? To love one another as God has loved us.

- Kindness is a conversion. Never forget that.

- Each one of you must be bread, broken and given, wine poured and shared.

- Great leaders are great servants. Go serve God, serve your family, serve your community.

- You will never fulfill the Scriptures (you read) until you are willing to live them.

- Your smile and an outstretched hand is the beginning of a miracle in the unspoken need of another's heart.

- Each morning, when you wake up, take Jesus by the hand. Ask Him: "Where do you want me to bring your kingdom?"

- If you see something that needs to be changed, change it. If you see someone who needs to be helped, help them. If you see something that needs to be done, do it. Be Jesus' hands, His heart, His feet, His mouth.

- Look after your feet, they must carry you a long way in this world and then all the way to the kingdom of God. (President George W. Bush used this quote in his acceptance speech.)

- Hold fast, go forward...fear nothing.

- A raging river never reflects the Sun (Son).

- Evil flourishes when good people don't speak.

- I couldn't do it (wash feet) unless I was convinced that I was touching Jesus.

- Each and every one is made in the image and likeness of Almighty God and the same hand that made them (the poor) is the same hand that made you and I. We are all poor, with a different set of circumstances.

- When someone is drowning, you don't throw them a life preserver, you get into the water with them.

- How can I help you?

- There can be no resurrection without a Calvary.

- In the evening of our lives, each one of us will be judged on one little thing...love, love, love...until it hurts.

- What is success? Success is remaining faithful to the will of God. What is the will of God? To love one another.

- We are responsible for the effort, not the outcome.

- Joy is the net of love in which we catch souls.

- Evil and death will never prevail; goodness and life always will.

- Don't pray too long, you'll get it wrong; we must go from prayer to action.

- We are called to be channels of God's peace, instruments of His love.

If this story has moved you, please feel free to contact Mary Jo Copeland at the following address:

Sharing and Caring Hands
525 North Seventh Street
Minneapolis, MN 55405
Web site: www.sharingandcaringhands.org

Worth Pondering

During my ten Mondays at Sharing and Caring Hands, I often heard the poor talk about Mary Jo. After receiving permission from Mary Jo, I invited several residents of Mary's Place, the transitional-housing complex, to share their thoughts on paper. Their reflections follow below. You may notice grammar mistakes and misspellings. Most of these quotes are unedited.

- "Mary Jo has made a difference in my life because she has provided a safe place for my family while we were homeless. She's helped me to put the Lord first in my life" (Sheila, married, mother of three small children).

- "She helps me do the right things in life. She help my family get better by helping me with shelter and food. She help my children to have respect… Now my children tells me that they love me. That mean a lot. I thought I lost my little girl, Victoria. She my first-born. Now I know that Victoria still loves me…" (April, single mother of three).

- "Out of all the help I received from any person or agency, Mary Jo is the only person who truly helped me. God sent me to Mary Jo…I needed time to rest. I needed peace and comfort. I needed to stop moving around all the time so my children could get settled in school. This year, my children all passed to the next grade level" (Sonya, thirty-six-year-old single mother, raising four children).

- "Mary Jo has brought us through one of the hardest times in our lives. She has restored our faith in people and God" (Pat, married mother of three children; husband lost his job after thirty years).

- "If it wasn't for her, I wouldn't be where I am now. My soul is at peace" (David, oldest son of six children, currently completing his education).

- "My boys and I are in a safe place and together, because of Mary Jo's love…" (Shirley, single mom with two sons).

- "She gave us a place to stay which is the nicest thing anyone has ever done for us. One of my sons is very sick and Mary Jo made him happy. When I get back on my feet, I will go and help others like she helped me" (Marlena, single mother of three sons, pregnant with a fourth child, recently left an abusive relationship).

- "Mary Jo helped me to realize that God does care for His children and that He never leaves us. One day, my children and I will return to this place and volunteer. We will be a source of blessing" (Audrey, single mother, lost job, evicted from apartment).

- "The county drop me and four kids off hear one day and left us hear one day. Mary Jo took me and the four kids in…the first night hear, we sat up and cried…me and four kids" (Larry, single father looking for a job).

- "Mary Jo wears hear heart on the outside of her shirt" (Yvette, single mother of six children).

- "Mary Jo has given me hope...now I feel like I can do anything I put my heart and mind to" (Tammy).

- "She taught me that it's alright to make mistakes, you just have to pick yourself right back up and keep moving forward..." (Sara, single mother of five trying to start a new life).

- "Mary Jo cares for the homeless...here, my family is safe" (Brenda, single mother of ten).

- "I came here to Minneapolis running from an abusive relationship. Mary Jo took me and my son in, jest like that. I finally have piece of mind" (Carol, single mother).

- "Mary Jo is an angel in disguise...for the first time in 13 years, I've been given the opportunity to start myself and my children's life over..." (Eloise, single mom).

- "She blesses the ones who doesn't have any place to go" (Shaveela, resident at Mary's Place).

- "Mary Jo looks on the inside of people. If she had not help us, I would had to send my children too different family members...she is holding us together. I just want a good life so I can educate myself and make a better life for my children..." (Janice, single mother of seven children).

- "I am from Mississippi, about 1000 miles away from Minnesota. Mary Jo give my family food, shelter, money, and love. Sometimes I can see it in her, that glow that Jesus had. She help me believe that one day Jesus will come back to get me and all His desperate people…" (Philip, father of twins and a four-year-old girl).

- "Mary Jo has given me something I haven't had since 1993; peace of mind" (Marion, single mother of three children, nursing student).

- "I was gonna take my life from the earth because I felt like I was worthless and no one cared weather I was dead or alive. Mary Jo put me in her arms and hug me and I never felt so secure and protected and loved and I mattered to her. She and Jesus Christ loved me and I had a reason to live because I was somebody" (Sheila, single mom, resident of Mary's Place).

- "I am a father that had no stability or self worth. I was lost within myself. Mary Jo guided me (and my family) back to the light. She helped us overcome depression and heal ourselves through prayer and meditation. She helped me to focus on right…" (Clarence, father).

Mission Statement

Sharing and Caring Hands is a compassionate response to the needs of the poor.

We are set up to be a safety net organization to help with whatever needs are not being met.

This includes, but is not limited to, providing meals, clothing, showers, shelter, transportation help, rent deposits, rent help, medical assistance, dental care, furniture, school expenses, funeral assistance, and other miscellaneous needs.

Sharing and Caring Hands provides these services with dignity, while affirming God's love for all His people, regardless of their circumstances. We reaffirm the self-worth of each individual and want to assist in that person's reaching his or her greatest potential.

Sharing and Caring Hands is an extension of the community to the desperate needs of the poor and exists as a vehicle for volunteers to commit their time and resources towards making a difference in the lives of others.

Sharing and Caring Hands stands as an emotional anchor and a beacon of hope to those who are alone, afraid, or in need.

About Mary Jo Copeland

(Note: This was written by Dick Copeland)

Mary Jo Copeland was born in Rochester, Minnesota, on October 23, 1942, the child of Gertrude and Woodrow Holtby. During the first six years of life, she lived at her paternal grandparents' house while "Woody" was in the service. Nellie doted on her granddaughter and took control of her upbringing while Gertrude continued to work.

The Holtbys looked at Mary Jo as their own little Shirley Temple and gave her every advantage, except a chance to bond with her mother or play with the neighborhood children.

When Woody came home from the service, they continued to live at his parents' house until Mary Jo was six, and then with the help of Woody's father, got a house of their own.

At this time, Mary Jo's brother John was born. All of a sudden Mary Jo's life changed completely. She went from a serene life where she was the center of attention to life with a mother she had never bonded with and a father she barely knew.

Woody came back from the war emotionally damaged and Gert was not much of a housewife. They fought constantly and the home was very chaotic. Over the years of growing up, Mary Jo had a hard time fitting in. She had not played with children much as a little child and lacked a lot of those social skills. She was afraid to bring friends home and she spent much of her time in her room to avoid the constant fighting. On top of this, her father constantly berated her and said, "You'll never amount to a row of beans. You can't do anything right." Her mother did not always make sure she bathed and the kids made fun of her at school.

Mary Jo did have a couple things going for her. She went to Annunciation Catholic School and the nuns taught her about God and his Blessed Mother. She turned to her religion for comfort, to the Blessed Mother as her surrogate mother, and she spent lots of time praying. She knew early on that she wanted to be a nun.

Mary Jo was a self-reliant little girl and tried to make the best of her life. In 1957, she met Dick Copeland at a dance, a meeting she engineered when she introduced herself by asking if he was Tom Kelly. He said no, but he asked her to dance and they have been dancing ever since. Dick and Mary Jo clicked right away and stayed high school sweethearts. Dick graduated from DeLaSalle in 1959 and went on to college; Mary Jo graduated from Holy Angels Academy in 1960 and went to work at St. Mary's Hospital.

Mary Jo married Dick on April 3, 1961. She decided to serve her beloved God and his Blessed Mother not by being a nun, but rather by being a good mother and wife. She was never accepted by Dick's family and her relationship with her own family was tense, but she was now totally in charge of her life and she loved it. She still felt the effects from her chaotic childhood and being told she would never amount to anything, but she was determined to overcome her past hardships.

Over the next sixteen years, Mary Jo and Dick had twelve children and two miscarriages. The sex of the children split evenly at six boys and six girls. With her last pregnancy, she hemorrhaged and had to have a hysterectomy. Her childbearing years were over. "What will I do now?" she thought.

During the years she raisied the kids, Mary Jo worked through many of the issues of her past. She even got her driver's license. By the time her youngest went off to school, she was ready to reach beyond her family. She always had her heart open to the call to serve God and she found that opportunity through volunteering.

She volunteered at Catholic Charities from 1982 to 1985, spoke in lots of churches, sensitizing people to the needs of the poor, and brought twenty-eight churches in to form the Branch Lunch Line.

In 1985, she started her own outreach to the poor called Sharing and Caring Hands at a storefront in downtown Minneapolis. Over the next seventeen years, Sharing and Caring Hands grew from a storefront to a campus for the poor, situated on seven acres of land on the edge of downtown. The campus includes a 27,000 square-foot main building that serves the needs of over a thousand people a day, including meals, clothing, food shelf, showers, medical and dental, and help with myriad other needs.

There is a 100,000 square-foot Mary's Place Transitional Shelter that houses 92 families, almost 500 people, most of them children. It has playgrounds, classrooms, and lots of things to help the residents make their transition to a new stable life. The campus also houses the Mary My Hope Children's Activity Center and the teen center.

Along the way, Mary Jo had to sue the city for the right

to build, but her determination and lots of public support won out. She got her approval.

Sharing and Caring Hands takes no United Way or government funding and charges no fees. Its multimillion-dollar budget and the entire campus was built with donations from the general public.

Mary Jo is an accomplished public speaker who has spent over twelve years speaking in churches and sensitizing people to the needs of the poor. From this effort came the volunteers, the financial support, and the recognition that was needed to enable the work to go on.

Over the years, Mary Jo's work has been featured in numerous articles, magazines, and television clips, and she has received many awards and much recognition. She spoke at the National Prayer Breakfast and was cited by President George W. Bush for her good works.

Mary Jo is currently working on raising thirty million dollars for a Children's Home she is building in Eagan, Minnesota. The Children's Home is the culmination of a two-year struggle to find a site and get approval. Her determination paid off again. Mary Jo intends to continue to work with the poor, people in need, and children until God calls her home to him.